FOR
WOMEN
who are called

BY
WOMEN
who have answered

FOR
WOMEN
who are called

BY
WOMEN
who have answered

KIM HANEY
and contributing authors

WORD AFLAME PRESS
WELDON SPRING, MO

Word Aflame Press
36 Research Park Court, Weldon Spring, MO 63304
pentecostalpublishing.com

Material from Elsy Cunningham, Linda Gleason, Joy Haney, Donna Hogue, Donna Linville, Debbie Saiz, Claudette Walker, and Bobbye Wendell is based on interviews and personal communication with the author and used by permission of the contributors. Some of the material has been edited for clarity and length.

Cover design by Joshua Rivas

Printed in the United States of America

26 25 24 23 22 21 20 19 18 17   1 2 3 4 5

Library of Congress Cataloging-in-Publication Data

Names: Haney, Kim, author.
Title: For women who are called by women who have answered / by Kim
    Haney ; and other contributors.
Description: Weldon Spring : Word Aflame Press, 2017. |
Identifiers: LCCN 2017035098 (print) | LCCN 2017035324 (ebook) |
    ISBN 9780757754791 () | ISBN 9780757754784 (alk. paper)
Subjects: LCSH: Women in church work. | Christian women--Religious
    life. | Vocation--Christianity.
Classification: LCC BV4415 (ebook) | LCC BV4415 .H36 2017 (print) |
    DDC 253.082--dc23
LC record available at https://lccn.loc.gov/2017035098

Contents

Foreword

by Nathaniel Haney

Those who have a desire and call to do something for the Lord Jesus Christ and His kingdom have a special place in the sight of the Almighty. When one considers that the world is now over seven billion in population, there are still relatively few who have shown a hunger and passion for the cause of the cross and our Lord who hung upon it. Even among those who answer this call, the level of drive, motives, and consecration varies greatly. One reason for this is due to what we feed our hearts and souls upon and what we have been exposed to. This is a large part of the molding process that personify who and what we become as we mature in ministry.

The apostle Paul makes a statement in I Corinthians 14:10, which states, "There are, it may be, so many kinds of voices in the world, and none of them is without signification." The simplicity of this statement states the fact that there is not one voice in a person's life that does not have some effect upon the mind and heart that hears it. Because of this, a person must determine what she will watch, hear, and read since these are channels that develop the beliefs and values that become the core of a person's being. It is true that every single voice in our lives will have some effect upon the person we are to become.

The book you hold in your hand is a book that has several voices, besides the author, and each one of these voices was influenced by older voices that are no longer with us. This means the voices of several generations of anointed and godly women, who were used by God and paid a tremendous cost in life, will be transmitted into the spirits, minds, and souls of those who read this book. With so many voices screaming into the ears of our ladies—from the secular side of modern feminism, denominations who have opened the door for women to fill unscriptural roles, to those who have taken the skin of Christianity and stuffed it with secular psychologies—many wonderful, God-fearing women are struggling to find their place and identity in relationship to the true call of God that rests upon their lives.

Seeing the storm that was brewing in the realm of the Spirit, I knew God would have some answers and chart a clear path for these special ladies who had been chosen to lead and minister in the twenty-first century. With many pastors and their wives praying, and many lady ministers searching for the balance of the biblical role of women in the church, I watched as the Lord began to place in my wife's heart the burden and content that was to eventually lead her to write this book. She understands an important principle of the kingdom of God: *One under authority has great authority.*

At the time of the writing of this book, she has walked beside me for over twenty-six years, and as the real world goes we have not always agreed on everything, yet she has respected me as the head of our home and I have respected her as the queen of our home. Her walk with God is far beyond that which she writes or speaks, with each morning when she rises she goes straight to her closet for prayer. Her passion to be involved with and facilitate a visit of the Holy Ghost in her personal life and among the ladies of Christian Life Center, or any meeting she is ministering in, has only increased with time. She has also surrounded herself with veteran lady ministers, many who now have crossed over to their reward on the other side. On most any day you can walk into our home when she is in the kitchen cooking or cleaning, or into the library were she's sewing or working on some project, and hear the voices of men and women of God from the past still preaching and ministering in the Haney home through recorded sermons.

This book is the sincere heart and soul of my wife and the life that she lives. This is the heartbeat that my four daughters and the women of my church are exposed to, which has made my home and the church that I pastor a safe and powerful place upon this earth. As a pastor and husband, there is not a price in monetary value that can be placed upon a wife, who has a calling, and knows her place in the Kingdom. Truly the price is far above rubies, gold, silver, and precious stones, but it will take eternity to tell the value and worth that many great women of God have contributed through the years to God's plan involving His kingdom.

by Linda Gleason

In a world that is hurtling headlong into eternity, a call rings forth from the portals of Heaven—the call to ministry. To men and women, young and old, the words of the prophet resound in this twenty-first century: "Whom shall I send, and who will go for us? Then said I, Here am I; send me" (Isaiah 6:8).

Kim Haney, as a young woman, felt the call. Her first mission was to five beautiful children who blessed their home. She began to teach the principles of the Word of God and the importance of drawing close to the Master, which was one of the significant steps in her path of ministry. As time has progressed, the call has led her to travel and preach to thousands of people, especially women. Her message leads to a closer walk with God, to hearing and following the voice of the Spirit.

For Women Who Are Called, by Women Who Have Answered is birthed from passion, experience, and faithfulness. Kim has tasted the ups and downs of life and has triumphed through the power of prayer and relationship with God. The mandate of Jesus still vibrates in our world, "Go ye into all the world, and preach the gospel to every creature" (Mark 16:15). Many are hearing His voice and are sincerely reaching to accomplish their purpose. Whether it be for teaching, preaching, or simply sharing your testimony; whether for your neighborhood, your city, or fields abroad, this book will help guide you in the fulfillment of your call. I encourage you to read it and follow a path that is open to all who are willing—the call to ministry.

Preface

If you are searching for a book that addresses and so-lidifies the fact that God does use women in various aspects of ministry, this is probably not the book for you. There are many great reads that specifically focus on the fact that God does indeed call women to various areas of ministry, and when working through the proper channels, they can be mightily used for the kingdom of God. The purpose and subject matter of this book are different.

This book is for the woman who has already felt the call of God and is asking, "What next?" Within these pages lies a carpenter's bag full of tools you will need for your journey. Some tools will require skill and patience and be harder to use than others, some tools you will use every day of your life, and others will be chosen only for certain projects and specific seasons along your journey.

As a skilled carpenter works side by side and gives hands-on training to his young protégé so he can prop-erly and effectively carry on the work, the voices that speak through these pages are from women who have given their lives to the call of God. The call of God has not been just a part of their life, but it has been their life. The treasures and wisdom they will pour into your soul through the pages of this book are priceless because a high price has been paid to obtain them. These are treasures that have been sown in tears, brokenness, and everything that produces a true anointing.

I caution you, dear reader. Do not read this book with your head, but read it with your heart and allow God to minister deep inside your spirit. Let the tears run down your cheeks when you read Bobbye Wendell's experience, heeding the call of God. Allow a spirit of sacrifice and hunger to grip your heart when you catch Joy Haney's heartbeat so you too can understand how to be an effective and anointed woman of God to your generation. Put yourself in the shoes of Donna Linville when the Lord began to test her sincerity and passion for ministry, and grasp Claudette Walker's understanding of where ministry all begins.

My deepest thanks to these precious women who have given so much of themselves to the Kingdom and for the many seeds they have sown, of which I am one. I am greatly humbled to have my life influenced by them and to be able to release these treasured truths into the next generation. May the Lord Jesus Christ work a spiritual transfer into the heart of every sincere reader, *For Women Who Are Called, by Women Who Have Answered*.

Special thanks to:

Elsy Cunningham	Donna Linville
Linda Gleason	Debbie Saiz
Joy Haney	Claudette Walker
Donna Hogue	Bobbye Wendell

About This Book

I didn't really understand what was happening at the time. Only fifteen years old, I tried to find my identity in high school, shuffling through friend circles, self-esteem issues, and society all together. Teenage years can be confusing and also cruel. People can hate you for being too pretty, too smart, too popular with the boys, looking different, being fat, being too skinny, or just because they want to pick on someone.

During this awkward season of my life, something began pulling inside me. A strong desire began to rise inside my spirit that I was unfamiliar with, and sadly, I had nobody around I could really talk to. Our house sat high on a hill overlooking the city of Tulsa, and my bedroom window is where it began to happen. Night after night, I would go to that window, open it just high enough so that God could hear me, get on my knees, and wait for the tears to begin their descent down my cheeks as I looked over the twinkling lights of the city. I'm sure if anyone ever noticed the windowpane, they would for sure suggest a leak somewhere due to the swollen wood panel that puddled my tears night after night.

Something internal that could not be seen or touched began to pull me away from everything a fifteen-year-old should be caught up with. Life became not so consumed with scavenging through my closet for hours, arranging my outfits for the next day. I began to think about souls. I began to think about the future. Jesus became more than just a story in a book as He would meet me at that window each night, and here, in this alone place, He became real to me. There in my bedroom, He became more than just an altar experience or religion. Jesus visited me every night. Not in a spooky ghost-like paranormal visitation, but I would feel His Spirit so strong as if He were literally standing in my room. I believe He was, not in bodily human form, but just as real as that.

I was not raised in a Pentecostal church. My parents were Southern Baptists until I was the age of ten. They were taught a *Search for Truth* home Bible study, and God gave them the revelation of the oneness of God and Jesus Name baptism. I was not raised in a preacher's home, for my father was in the oil and gas business all my life. But God saw something in this young girl's heart that desired to know Him, a hunger to pursue Him beyond anything else, and from this desire began a relationship that has kept me through all life has thrown my way.

Looking out that bedroom window across that vast city, through my tears I would cry out to God, "Please, place me in the middle of revival; that's all I ask. Wherever that may be, whomever it's with, that's where I want to be, God. I want to live in the middle of where Your Spirit is being poured out!" Ministry never even crossed my mind. I was naïve to all the Christian politics and religious views that many times accompany the desire to be involved in ministry. All I knew was that I loved the Lord and I wanted the future of my life to be consumed with His purpose—wherever that road may take me.

For three years this internal drawing continued, and trust me, the enemy tried to divert me many times from what I could not understand. I had my struggles through high school trying to fit in and be accepted, but that tugging at my heart never stopped. Somehow I knew something was happening deep inside, but I had no one to talk to who could help me understand what was taking place.

In 1989 I graduated from high school. I had a close friend who attended Christian Life College in Stockton, California, and she had briefly mentioned that I should come to room with her that next year. California was a long way from Oklahoma, but that tugging and pulling inside kept telling me this is where I needed to be. Of course, this is when the next opposition came.

I have a wonderful father who has always provided well for our family but did not even consider entertaining the idea of his daughter attending a Bible college. He had plans for me, and those plans included a reputable college and a secular degree behind my name. The red carpet of temptation was rolled out when a brand-new sports car with a phone installed (okay, this was before cell phones) was included in the package.

It made sense for me to accept this generous offer and go with the flow of what was expected of me from my family, but that pulling and tugging inside became more powerful than monetary or material worth. May I insert this one statement: if something of natural gain or monetary status can pull you away from what you think is a call of God, most assuredly you were never truly called in the first place. The call of God will take priority above anything that status, prestige, or any level of importance may offer. Ask Moses. Ask Daniel. And trust me, you will be tested. Just like Hezekiah, God will leave you to yourself at times in order to test you, to see all that is in your heart. The purpose of the test is to see if He can trust you to covet, love, and protect the highest calling known to man and to know how loyal you will be to the calling.

I came to this juncture in the road, not wanting to disrespect my dad but feeling the intensity of God's calling me to Bible college. So I began to pray. I asked the Lord to change my dad's heart and to let him accept the fact I wanted to go to Bible college. This was a test of my faith, knowing it would take an absolute miracle for God to change my dad's heart. It was also a test of my calling. God was watching how I responded to my authority— even though there was complete lack of understanding. Was I going to make it work by my own powers and use the ticket, *I am now an eighteen-year-old adult and can make my own choices whether you agree or not,* or was I going to really trust God enough to know He was big enough to make a way if I was truly in His will? It came down to where I had to believe God really did hear my prayers.

It did not happen overnight. In fact, only a couple weeks before the semester started, I found myself, along with my parents, on the long road to California. God proved Himself to me in a way I will never forget when He touched the heart of my dad. I didn't know if I would be there only one year, two years, or what my future held; I only knew I had to take it a day at a time. That's how God operates, one day at a time. It would sure be nice if He would stretch out His plan before our eyes and let us know what our future holds and what steps to take down the road, but He doesn't. There would be no need for faith if that happened. There would be no need to hear His voice or no reason to seek His face if we were able to see our futures laid out, but there is one thing He does let us hear, His voice. He said His sheep know His voice.

I had absolutely no intentions of dating anyone in Bible college. As I mentioned before, I was naïve to many aspects of ministry and all the politics that were involved. I just wanted to dive into the things of God, like prayer, fasting, and understanding the Word of God. Throughout that year my eyes were focused on my purpose until they got diverted by a special young man halfway through my freshman year. I had in my mind what type of husband I wanted, but that would happen far in the future—or so I thought.

I knew I wanted a young man who was consumed with the things of God, lived a life of prayer, and was noncompromising. I found that and more when I fell in love with Nathaniel Haney. Twenty-six years later (at the time of this writing), that man has not changed but has become more committed and in love with Jesus.

I told you my story to say this: I never dreamed I would someday be a minister's wife and college instructor, much less a licensed minister. Never in my wildest imagination would I have guessed I would be the pastor's wife of Christian Life Center, the greatest church on the face of the planet (okay, in my opinion). Every time I stand in front of a classroom full of Christian Life College students, it still brings tears to my eyes to think that God would allow me this privilege to affect the lives of future ministers because I still realize that I am nobody. I had nothing to offer God except willingness. I have no Pentecostal pedigree, no impressive college degree behind my name, and no great talents or abilities that would ever qualify me for such a calling. If God can use me, He can use you.

For the past twenty years, I have had the privilege of interacting with young women from all over the world who have the same passion and inner voice drawing them to a place unfamiliar. Some of them I meet when I travel; others connected through Christian Life College and beyond. For the most part they have the same questions, the same fears, and the same passion and come in need of direction. Even though I have been involved in ministry for over twenty-five years, I find myself not qualified to write the totality of this book. There are far more women who, like they say, "Have more corn in the crib"; in other words, have many more years of experience and much more wisdom.

God has allowed me to be influenced by some of the greatest women of our time, and for this I am deeply grateful. He has brought friends into my life, whom I used to watch from afar in deep respect and awe of their walk with God, and allowed them to speak into my life and shape who I have become. I am deeply humbled by this and yet so thankful. I have asked several of them to become vulnerable and willing to speak into your life through this book as if you're interacting one-on-one. They will share things with you that would be spoken after a good prayer meeting or powerful move of God when your spirit is open to receive. They will speak things that are intimate and cannot be shared with just anyone. The treasures of advice, the pouring out of their experiences, and revealing of pain that many times involve the call, will no doubt either encourage you or make you think twice about your calling.

As I mentioned before, this book is not going to address the question, "Does God use women in ministry?" This has been untouched mainly due to the fact that anyone who reads the Scripture understands without doubt there is a place for women in the kingdom of God. The pages of this manuscript are for the woman who is already feeling a call from God and wants to learn how to be effective in her generation. My prayer is that this book will be a voice in a troubled and somewhat confused world of religion and "ministry mentalities" that have bled into the thinking of the church, to give a clear and certain sound of what it really means to be a woman who is called of God.

Remember this one thing: "Ministry is not an occupation that can just be chosen. Ministry is not a job description. Ministry is a divine call." I bid you Godspeed.

—Kim Haney

1 | *Knowing the Call*

She sat in the leopard-print chair in my office. She was a beautiful, passionate young lady who had come a long way from home to attend Bible college in California. She made an appointment to talk with me, and although I wasn't sure I knew what it was about, I had an idea. I could tell there was a tinge of nervousness as she made her way into my office, so we made some small talk about missing home, her favorite classes, and Mexican-food Wednesdays in the Student Center. As the conversation moved into a more serious mode, she looked at me and said, "Sister Haney, I feel the Lord has called me to ministry." We discussed this calling for a few minutes until I turned and asked her if there was a certain direction she was feeling. Without any hesitation, she turned her face toward me with complete confidence and stated, "The Lord is calling me to be a preacher. I *want* to preach."

I don't know if she really noticed the complete look of shock on my face. It was not due to the fact she was called to ministry but more about the initial goal. It was like she had been going to college to be a veterinarian, and one morning she woke up to the realization she wanted to be a brain surgeon. Just as a student chooses his or her degree program, the call to ministry was being viewed in the same way—through the eyes of a secular mentality.

Sadly, there are too many who unintentionally view the call to ministry as a sort of employment or vocation opportunity where you can pick and choose how you want to fit into the kingdom and choose the course of exactly how God will use you. Maybe their lives were deeply affected while listening to someone who operated under the anointing, and with sincerity of heart, they make the choice to follow in that pursuit. But the call to ministry is just that; it's a sacred calling that goes forth from a supernatural source called the Spirit of God and should not be confused with a secular mentality initiated by secular goals.

Some great spiritual secret or deep theological enlightenment does not take place when that call goes forth, but the mission does take hold of your spirit in a way that won't let go. A call of God will cause you to turn corners in your life you can point back to years later and say, "That is the spot on the carpet," or "there is the corner," or "there is the place where it was birthed." You never forget the place and time and way that it happened because it's *that* life transforming. The call of God never leaves, it never wavers, and it never fades or fizzles out but just keeps getting stronger and more vocal as it speaks into your soul day after day.

KNOWING THE VOICE OF GOD

That familiar, distant voice will speak into your spirit over and over again. We can all be moved internally when a powerful message has been preached, and you find yourself falling over an altar as your spirit connects to the heart of God. But a calling goes beyond an altar experience. Although it can be birthed there, it is something that never finds release but with time becomes stronger and clearer. It will pop up at the strangest times and most awkward places. It will descend upon you when you're in a restaurant sitting at a table filled with friends, and out of nowhere the persistent voice of God will come knocking on the door of your heart until you have to excuse yourself to go outside to get alone with God. You will find yourself sitting in a classroom, trying to concentrate on the lecture of your instructor, but the voice of God is speaking louder as it pulls at your soul. Just like an infant recognizes its mother's voice among all others, so will your soul recognize when God is calling your name.

The Bible makes it clear that the call of God upon one's life is not an occupational choice or decision that can be made by desire alone. The Scriptures make reference to the role of the Old Testament high priest when the writer of Hebrews made this statement:

> And no man taketh this honour unto himself, but he
> that is called of God, as was Aaron. (Hebrews 5:4)

This office comes with a high degree of responsibility, but notice something about this verse. It makes mention of Aaron being the one who was called of God, but Aaron did not preach at all. The pulpit ministry was not part of his calling, yet the Scriptures classify him as a man who had a call of God upon his life. Sometimes we limit the calling to certain offices or positions that in turn will limit God's ability to use us in the way He desires. Aaron learned to know the voice of God, and with that ability came direction for his specific calling.

To stand before men as God's ambassador must require a calling from above, but if someone does not respect this sacred calling and is moved by self-will, other people's perspectives, popularity, or even their own desire, the Lord will say to them, "I sent them not, nor commanded them: therefore they shall not profit this people at all, saith the LORD" (Jeremiah 23:32). That, my friend, would be a dangerous place.

Isaiah did not jump at the opportunity to minister until he had a firm confirmation, along with a supernatural sign, that the Lord was calling him. He did not make a move toward ministry until he had been specially visited by the Lord, and when this did happen, he felt qualified for his ministry.

> Also I heard the voice of the Lord, saying, Whom shall I send, and who will go for us? Then said I, Here am I; send me. (Isaiah 6:8)

The call of God will burn in your heart.
In Luke 24, Jesus had just resurrected from the dead, but many of His dedicated disciples who followed

His ministry did not believe it. We come to the scene of two of Jesus' disciples taking a walk and talking together. I'm sure they were trying to put all the pieces of the puzzle together as two men who had lived through a tornado—their entire world had been ripped apart. This Jesus, whom they had given their lives to and walked away from everything else, was now dead, but His death brought the burial of their dreams and futures as well.

> And they talked together of all these things which had happened. And it came to pass, that, while they communed together and reasoned, Jesus himself drew near, and went with them. But their eyes were holden [blinded] that they should not know him. (Luke 24:14–16)

Out of nowhere Jesus appeared to them, but they only saw Him as a stranger who had come into town as He joined their discussion and listened to their disappointments. As they walked, they began to discuss the Scriptures. Jesus reprimanded them for their lack of faith and reminded them of the promises of God that were released by the mouths of the prophets. As the day came to a close, Jesus sat with these men and ate bread with them. After this,

> their eyes were opened, and they knew him; and he vanished out of their sight. And they said one to another, *Did not our heart burn within us,* while he talked with us by the way, and while he opened to us the scriptures? (Luke 24:31–32, my emphasis)

A certain feeling comes when Jesus is talking Spirit-to-spirit with His people. Luke described this inner connection as a "burning." *Ellicott's Commentary for English Readers* states this burning was a "continuous and not a momentary state or act." It's an inner burning that won't let go no matter how hard you try to suppress it or ignore it. This desire does not fade with time. The call of God takes you to the place where nothing else matters. The esteem and favor of the world's acceptance and walls filled with fancy plaques of degrees fade into the background as the call of God burns inside of your soul. Others around you can move forward and reach for certain esteemed occupations, life goals, levels of education, and success in the world's view, but that burning inside never ceases its voice in your life.

Claudette Walker shares how she began to learn to hear the voice of the Lord:

> I personally believe that the Lord calls us just as He called His disciples. He spoke to them. When they heard His voice, they were then able to leave their fishing nets and tax table, giving up *all* to follow His call.
>
> Jesus said in John 10:27, "My sheep hear my voice, and I know them, and they follow me." Learning to hear the voice of the Lord is a process, but God is well able to speak in such a way that even a teenager, such as I was, can clearly hear His voice. I believe that we need to be able to go back and remind ourselves of our call because the enemy will cause us to doubt that God ever called us. I urge you also to pray for a confirmation to the call.

God will send others who see and sense God's call on your life, but only you can really know. Record the words they speak to you in a journal and ask God to confirm to you His perfect will.

Next to my Bible, which is the greatest treasure in my home, are pages of words from the Lord spoken to my own heart or through others. I have these words also carefully dated. . . . I keep these pages in the front of a notebook that I use when I preach His Word. When I step to that pulpit, the pages of every message I speak is placed over the many pages of *rhemas* (spoken words of God) that were spoken to my heart and through others. I simply remind the Lord, "I am standing on Your call and on all Your words You have spoken to me through the years. I do not trust in my own abilities. Nor do I trust in my preparation. I stand on *my calling* and on every word You have given me since that time concerning my calling."

Since I base my entire confidence in ministry on this, I know of nothing more important than knowing God has called us as we have listened to His voice speak into our spirits. Obviously, since His voice is our ultimate foundation and ongoing structure of ministry, we need to have a passion to hear it. God will train you through much fasting and prayer to hear Him clearly. I would give up every possession, friends, and my health to know and to be able to hear His voice. The world of this generation is so noisy today with the sounds of social media, videos of entertainment, music, even the words of people we love. Sometimes you have to get to the place where you must quiet the noise! God does not scream nor is He rude to interrupt. He speaks in a still, small voice to those who long to hear His words. All true ministry is simply relaying to people the words of the Lord. However, I cannot give what I do not hear.

You will not find Jesus in the crowds of people, and you will not find Him when you're surrounded by voices on every side. You will find Him in the stillness of the night. You will find Him in a solitary place where you seclude yourself away from all others and seek for Him alone. Those are the places He will speak to you. Those are the times you will learn to hear His voice. It's the dark and lonely prayer closet; it's the times of loneliness and isolation. You will hear the voice of the Lord when all other voices are silenced and you find yourself in a place where you can listen.

The voice of God speaks to our spirits.

> For as many as are led by the Spirit of God, they are the sons of God. . . . The Spirit itself beareth witness with our spirit, that we are the children of God. (Romans 8:14, 16)

This means God will enlighten and guide us through our human spirits. Because God communes and talks with us through our spirit, it is vitally important we keep our spirits tuned to the Holy Ghost through prayer and praying in the Holy Ghost. Many times, young women will see the bright lights of a pulpit ministry or be greatly ministered to through a woman minister and not understand the channel in which the call of God flows. They will begin to desire a place of ministry just due to the fact they had been affected personally by someone who operated under the calling. Sometimes we judge these things by our own physical senses, and nowhere does God mention that He will guide us through our physical senses, our powerful altar experiences, some well-meaning person prophesying our future, or even the natural realm and feelings that we become so dependent upon.

Solomon described the spirit of a person as the candle (or the lamp) of the Lord:

> The spirit of man is the candle of the LORD, searching all the inward parts of the belly. (Proverbs 20:27)

The word for "spirit" in Hebrew literally means "breath." This means God will guide you, talk to you, and breathe on you through your spirit. "The candle of the LORD" is given to us as an inward light and guide. Peter calls this inward person the "hidden person of the heart" (I Peter 3:4, NASB). When we become more spirit-conscious than experience- or physical-conscious, we can begin to hear what the Spirit of God is saying to the spirit inside us. The more spirit-conscious we become, the more real the leading of the Lord will become to us. Job described how the voice of God speaks to the spirit inside a person:

> But it is the spirit in a person, the breath of the Almighty, that gives them understanding. (Job 32:8, NIV)

Inside this inward, spirit person, God will guide us. This spirit person is made alive and sensitive to the voice of God through prayer and getting alone with God (which we will discuss later in this book). In I Corinthians 14, Paul addressed how this operates in the lives of God's people:

> For if I pray in an unknown tongue, my spirit prayeth, but my understanding is unfruitful. (I Corinthians 14:14)

When you are filled with the Holy Ghost with the evidence of speaking in other tongues as the Scripture states, a special connection takes place between your human spirit and the Spirit of God. Paul said when you pray in these unknown tongues, your spirit is reaching out and connecting with the Spirit of God. The apostle was trying to convey to us that God will guide us and commune with us through our spirit.

Bobbye Wendell makes this statement regarding her first experiences with feeling the call of God:

> When I got the Holy Ghost, the spirit of intercession came upon me, and I had never experienced anything like it. When I went into intercession, I saw a vision in my mind; it was a huge, turning world and my heart felt like it was going to move out of my body and move toward that world. After I had this experience, I went on a fast, and during this fast the Lord spoke to me out of His Word, Psalm 68:31:
>
> > Princes shall come out of Egypt; Ethiopia shall soon stretch out her hands unto God. (Psalm 68:31)
>
> The Lord welded that message and Scripture into me. I was sitting at a table, and the Scripture

literally began to glare at me. I closed my Bible and thought, *I don't even know what that means,* but when I opened the Bible again, it fell open to the same page. Then it frightened me. When I saw the word "Ethiopia," I thought, *I don't even know where that place is.* There was a magazine on the table, and when I opened it I saw a page with an article about Ethiopia. From that day forward, Ethiopia became a part of me, and God has never released me from that because I have never asked Him to.

When we talk about a call, the definition means a summons. God summons us. We either answer it or we don't. You can either go in the door and accept it or stand just inside the door the rest of your life and miss what God has by not stepping through and exploring anything. You can say, "I have a license, I am a preacher, I am a minister," and you might preach a little message or sermon, but it will never have fulfillment. When a connection is really made, you will see the fruits by the choices you make. God has called many, but few are chosen.

The late Kenneth E. Hagin said it this way: "*Feeling* is the voice of the body, *reason* is the voice of the soul (or mind), and *conscience* is voice of the spirit."

How many times are we moved to make decisions by what we feel? How many times do we make life decisions by what is comfortable for our flesh? How many times do we determine our destiny based on logic? I will be the first to admit I've been guilty of them all, and they have gotten me into regretful situations. The Scripture states that the Spirit of

God bears witness with *our spirits*—not our feelings or thoughts or the situation surrounding us at that time.

To better understand how our spirit speaks to us, let me ask you a question. Have you ever said something to someone or spoke something that was not entirely true, and immediately you felt a tree trunk in your throat as the reality of conviction settled in? That is your spirit speaking to you. It's your spirit, or that inner voice, that is convicting you of what you said.

> Know ye not that ye are the temple of God, and that the Spirit of God dwelleth in you? (I Corinthians 3:16)

> And what agreement hath the temple of God with idols? for ye are the temple of the living God; as God hath said, I will dwell in them, and walk in them; and I will be their God, and they shall be my people. (II Corinthians 6:16)

If God is dwelling and living inside our spirit, that is the place where He will commune and talk to us; this is the place the call will go forth. Our part is taking the time to listen to Him. When you set yourself alone with God in prayer and learn to hear His voice, you will not question the direction He has for your life. But many don't want to make the time to set themselves apart to the Lord.

Some people seek God's direction in strange ways or seek Him through methods that worked for one generation but are not intended for the next. For instance, it's not always a wise thing to place a "fleece" before the Lord, especially when it's a decision that could alter or change the course of your life. The Scripture did not say that the sons of God are *led by the fleeces of God*—this was a method used by men to confirm God's will prior to the Holy Spirit baptism.

Yes, Gideon did set out a fleece before the Lord when he needed direction, but you and I are living in a new covenant where we have the actual Spirit of the Lord living inside us. You never see anyone in the New Testament or any of the disciples laying fleeces before God. People use these things because it can be easier than waiting on God. It's easier to say, "Lord, You open the door if You want it opened and close it if You want it closed, and I will just sit here and wait." We are so busy and caught up in a time-con-scious culture that "waiting on the Lord" is foreign to us. It is inconvenient to our flesh and a hindrance to our schedules.

We have voices speaking and talking into our lives at all hours of the day through cell phones, emails, texts, and the Internet as we are pressured to be places all hours of the day. Our minds become so clouded with all this junk that if we don't set aside a specific *time* and *place* to meet with God every day, we will not be able to hear what His voice sounds like.

When a woman of God learns to hear the voice of the Lord, God will use her mightily. And you learn to hear His voice by spending time with Him. The world won't be behind you waving flags of support, you won't always have a whole host of close friends who are supporting you in your call, or a squad of cheerleaders on the sidelines. Many times, your family members will not be there to support you, but that is all right. You can stand before the Lord and do whatever it is He has called you to do because of the peace that comes to confirm your purpose.

Bobbye Wendell makes this statement about her calling:

> The true call of God is without repentance. It never leaves. Whether we answer the call or not, it falls upon us, but we can never say *I had* a call. I think there needs to be some distinction when it comes to a call to preach and a call to ministry, and it would help many women to decipher between the two. There is a call to preach and there is a call to serve. Many times it begins with a call to serve, and as God proves you and you prove yourself to Him that He can trust you, it can develop into something more.
>
> We live in a generation where women want to jump into the pulpit. They have their agenda. They have their plan. Many of them don't want to do what we did—live a sacrificial lifestyle. Women who are involved in business, politics, and leadership have multiplied in this culture, and there seems to be a "glass ceiling" above women.
>
> The most tragic mistake that women can make is to feel they are in competition with men. That is the worst thing a woman can do if she feels a call to minister the Word of God. There was something born in me at the altar that made me want to give back to the work of God. I remember looking down at my hands and thinking, *My hands are clean and I want to give them back to the Lord. I want them to serve God.* I thought if I could do something for the Kingdom, even if it was getting

my hands dirty by working hard, I just wanted to give something back to God. I didn't understand anything about church culture or church politics, but the Lord gave me a testimony. I didn't think about what I was called to do; I just wanted to do something for God.

A certain level of contentment comes when you fall in line with God's plan for your life. When there is a true call of God upon your life, you will never be content, you will never be satisfied, you will never be happy until you find out what God wants you to do and then do it with all your heart.

No one can tell you that you're called.
I have one son who is eighteen years old at the time of this writing. Joshua has always had a heart for the things of God and, even at the young age of fourteen, began seeking the Lord in the early morning hours, developing a prayer life. He is disciplined, a hard worker who has held a job since he was sixteen, and has never given us any problems. But I fear for him. He comes from a lineage of great men and women of God who, without doubt, have been called and used mightily in their lifetime in the honorable place of ministry. He, no doubt, has felt unrelenting pressure to follow suit and do what everyone expects of him.

Too many well-meaning people have pressured their way into ministry or maybe have been pushed and compelled into a certain position because it is expected of them, because of the family lineage or heritage, or because a parent is trying to live his or her life through the child. These are situations that are real, and you have to be aware of them because *only you* can know if God has called you to this high honor of ministry. If you do not know it, nobody else can tell you.

Maybe some young lady who is reading this right now is unadvisedly about to take a step that would lead to a negative outcome. Do not take a step until you have prayed and received a clear answer and direction from God alone regarding your call to ministry and there is a witness from those who are authorities in your life. Your parents cannot tell you you're called. Not your pastor. Not your best friend, your boyfriend, or husband. People can be used to confirm what you're already feeling, but they should not be the ones to choose this road for you.

My husband and I have never told any of our five children he or she is called to ministry. Although that is my personal desire for all of them and I have raised them to be prepared for this calling if God does decide this direction for their lives, I cannot call them into ministry. All that matters to me is they have a relationship with Jesus, walk with God, and have a love for truth. Sometimes well-meaning saints will make comments such as, "You're next in line," or "I'm looking at our next pastor," which is meant as a compliment. However, they do not really understand the pressure they are placing upon a young person to "perform" as expected. The church is not made up of a family dynasty. No one (however wonderful they may be) can tell you that God is calling you to ministry. The exception would be someone confirming what you are already feeling, but only you can truly know if there is a supernatural call going forth on your life.

God chose Moses, but He did not choose any of Moses' sons, God chose Joshua to be Moses' successor. God chose Eli to ministry, but He did not choose any of Eli's sons, due to their negative choices. God called Saul, but He did not choose Jonathan, who was the crown prince of Israel. Instead, He chose David, a simple shepherd boy.

Being involved with Christian Life College for several years, I have taken note of the hundreds of precious young adults who have come through this college, and sometimes I have been heartbroken at certain situations. In a few instances I have watched young people, some of them pastors' kids, break under the pressure of what is expected of them and literally run the other way to the extreme. They become bitter, angry, and resentful toward God, their parents, and the ministry—all because they were being pushed and pressed in a direction where they either were not called to fulfill or had not heard the voice of God for themselves.

I have also witnessed the opposite. If a person tries to push and make herself a preacher, a teacher, a pastor, or a minister, and does not have a divine calling, not only will she be ineffective, but she can bring great harm upon the kingdom of God. People who are not truly called will create saints who abhor the church, develop mistrust and a cynical attitude toward the ministry, become angry and bitter toward the God whom this person misrepresents, and will usually end up turning their backs on the church and the Lord altogether—all because someone stepped out of the will of God.

I have witnessed this through the years, and if you're honest, I'm sure you have too. A woman who is called to ministry will be dealing with spiritual forces and must have the anointing upon her head as the seal of God we read about in the Old Testament. There is a big responsibility to stand before an audience and proclaim that you have heard from Almighty God and stand before them with a Word from the Lord! Hear me, young lady; don't let anyone *tell you* that you have a call to ministry upon your life. There may be some well-meaning people who love you and see potential inside you, but no one on this earth can tell you that you are called. This is something that can come from God alone.

A God-called minister is not a minister because someone lays hands upon her, anoints her with oil, and prays over her, or because she has the blessing of the bishop or pastor, but ministry comes through the call of the Spirit. That ministry calling is vindicated and confirmed through leadership, the power of God, and the anointing that rests upon that person when she ministers.

By now, you may be wondering, "I'm not sure if I really am called to ministry." Good. That is what I want you to be asking. This generation must have people who are full of faith in their God and in their calling no matter what crosses their path. The people who can face the greatest of trials and still become powerful and effective develop from knowing without a doubt that God's call and anointing is upon them. You will go through some rough times, and some seasons in your life will become so void and dry that they will make you question your calling. Ask Elijah.

You cannot just wake up one morning, decide to change majors, enroll in a seminary, and make the choice to become a female minister. Ministry is not a choice, nor do you become a minister just because you have a minister's license. Ministry is not a job description, and obtaining a minister's license should not be viewed in the same way as earning another degree or hanging a plaque on your wall as an accomplishment. Ministry is not an employment opportunity, but it is a divine calling that goes forth from the Spirit of the Lord.

Donna Linville tells us how she first knew God was calling her to ministry:

> My personal place of calling happened when I was about nine years old. At that age I didn't really understand the voice of God, and it was my mother who actually helped me to understand that it really was God who was speaking to me. I do know this one thing: God will speak to a child. In a simple service, I was standing at the altar during prayer. A thought went through my mind, and I told the thought to my mother. I know now the Lord was speaking to my spirit, but as a child I didn't understand this. The thought was, "Mom, I feel like the Lord said I was going to marry a minister."

My mother, with wisdom said, "Donna, I don't believe it's your flesh that wants you to be in ministry. I don't think the devil wants you to be married to a minister. So whose voice do you think spoke that to you?" I knew it was God, for only God would ask me to give my life to Him. That one seed continued to grow through the consistency of being in church services and being privileged to be in services with missionaries, Bible college students, and anointed choirs who would come through my hometown. The voice of God would continue to speak to me through the missionary presentations as the tears would fall down my cheeks and I would cry for the lost overseas. God started growing that love for the ministry as the Spirit started wooing me. I also was blessed to have mentors around me to help me understand that God was wooing me. Mentors in my life such as Sunday school teachers and my pastor helped me form that calling as they began to use me in little things. The call of God began little by little, but as time went on, it began to progress until it would not let go.

It is vitally important that you know the voice of the calling for yourself. This is something you must know, for no one else on the planet can tell you that you are called of God. But when you know it, nothing can pull you from it—no trial, storm, or dry, deserted season. There is an intense, constant-pulling desire for the work of God. There must be an irresistible, overwhelming craving and thirst for telling others what God has done in your own life. This desire never leaves or wavers; it's a passion that stays alive even when tests and trials come into our lives.

Those who are truly called have a solid love for truth, and compromise is far from their ears. They are not afraid to walk alone. They are not bound by what others think of them nor pressured to be in the circles of popularity. A woman who is called by God must revisit this statement over and over again throughout her lifetime: *It's not what others know, but it's what God sees.* Having that truth buried deep inside your heart will make you an effective vessel of honor.

Marriage: Taking on the mantle of the call
Every other year I am honored to teach an elective course, "Marriage and Family," at Christian Life College. It's a fun class and one of my favorites because the classroom is always filled to capacity with a mixture of guys and girls who are all in this anxious season of wondering who they might end up marrying. It always cracks me up inside as the semester begins and I scan the classroom filled with new students. You can always pick them out. The giggling girls (and sometimes guys) who rush to grab the front-row seats sending forth the message loud and clear they are here to earn their "MRS" degree, and they are ready to learn how to obtain this degree. Some students in the mix really secretly want to know more about this fascinating subject but refrain from exuding too much display of excitement in fear of sending out the message they are desperate (or even looking) for a spouse. Then there are the really fun ones whom

I love to engage in classroom discussions. These are usually young men who are trying to act "too cool" because they are *so not interested* in this marriage thing because as far as they are concerned, they are the greatest thing that has hit the campus.

I take this class seriously due to this fact: If you choose to marry, your choice in who you marry is the most important choice you will make in your entire life (of course, second in place behind the choice to serve the Lord). Your spouse will affect every area of your life and ministry. We discuss the importance of dating God first, making sure each life is founded upon the rock of an everyday, consistent prayer life. You will find out quickly that the magical land of married life is definitely not Disneyland and that Prince Charming and beautiful Cinderella were not designed and not capable of fulfilling every void in your life—only Jesus can do that.

Elsy Cunningham talks about the call of a minister's wife:

> Even though there are many hindrances for women who feel a call to ministry, one of the greatest hindrances is that many ministers' wives are not transparent and feel as if they need to put on a façade. In being transparent, we must ask the Lord to give wisdom and balance in what to share and what not to share. Many young women see only the prominence, the spotlight, and the privilege that come with ministry, and it appears, at times, this is the greatest attraction for some to feel a call to ministry. If ministers' wives were more transparent about what ministry entailed,

then young ministers' wives might stop and evaluate their motives before becoming involved in ministry. Ministry is being a servant. It is work. It is loving people and helping people, no matter the task.

A minister's wife must be approachable, real, and down-to-earth so that people feel comfortable around her in a respectful manner. Being unapproachable and artificial is a hindrance to young women wanting to be in the ministry. People want a minister's wife who is genuine.

The first words out of Adam's mouth when he woke up from his God-induced coma were not, "Hey, wife, what's for dinner?" or "Wow, what an attractive woman God blessed me with!" But the first words out of his mouth were:

> And the LORD God caused a deep sleep to fall upon Adam, and he slept: and he took one of his ribs, and closed up the flesh instead thereof; and the rib, which the LORD God had taken from man, made he a woman, and brought her unto the man. And Adam said, This is now bone of my bones, and flesh of my flesh: she shall be called Woman, because she was taken out of Man. (Genesis 2:21–23)

Adam knew there was more than just a pretty face staring back at him or a gourmet chef ready to fix him an apple pie. He said Eve was "bone of my bones, and flesh of my flesh." This meant Adam saw that Eve was in her person, her purpose, and her mind every way suitable to be his companion to help him fulfill his calling in life. No doubt, the physical attraction was there, but the union was not based on what she looked like or how talented she was. The union was based on Eve's being equally yoked in purpose and calling with Adam.

Adam did not name her Eve, but her name was *Ishah,* which is a Hebrew word for "woman" because she came out of *Ish,* which is the Hebrew word for "man." In other words, he distinguished her from the rest of the animals in the garden. In that whole phrase and statement, Adam said, "She is different from the other stuff I've been giving names to these last few days, for she is one of me." He knew in his human spirit that God had given him a helper who shared his heartbeat, desires, and passions, and she helped him fulfill the purpose of God for their lives. She was bone of his bone, flesh of his flesh, or, "She is one being with me."

It went beyond the physical similarities. She thought like him. She had the same desires as he did. They worked together to fulfill their mission in the garden each day. He didn't have his own agenda or call of God while she had her vocation she wanted to pursue, but she was bonded with him in passion, calling, and purpose.

This is important to grasp! Young lady, if God has laid upon your heart a burden for the mission field or you feel a specific calling to a specific area of ministry, any prospective future husband should have the same type of calling upon his life. A mutual call is important for young men too, but the reason I'm addressing the young ladies is because whomever you choose to marry, you will be required by God to submit to your husband, not only to his authority but also to his calling in life. As a helpmeet or helper to that man, your calling will thrive and flourish, but if you marry unequally yoked in calling, it will bring much frustration, discouragement, and inner regrets because God's plan is for God-called husband-and-wife teams to be linked together not only in doctrine but also in calling.

Several years ago, a particularly spiritual young lady attended Christian Life College. She was a prayer warrior, had a great hunger for the things of God, had a distinct calling for missions, and carried a great burden for this call. She ended up marrying a good young man who was a hard worker and a great father to their kids. But he didn't share her burden, and he didn't have a call upon his life for ministry.

She thought she could change him once they were married and that he would join her in her burden for overseas ministry, but that never happened. (Most of the time, it's not God's design or plan for it to work that way.) I watched from a distance as she did her best to try to push him into positions of ministry in their local church, trying to make a preacher out of him. All it ended up doing was bringing resentment and friction into their marriage. To this day, she has shelved the call of God upon her life and is just sitting on a church pew somewhere, not feeling satisfied.

I have to caution you. Just because a young man is saved, single, filled with the Holy Ghost, attends church, sings in the choir, and runs the aisles does not mean that you are equally yoked. If he catches your eye because of the name-brand suit he wears, how well he can sing or play an instrument, the way he can move a crowd by his preaching, his impressive family lineage, or even how handsome he is, you might get home and find out you have married one of the beasts of the field. It's a difficult time of life because so many single young ladies never realize that a marriage goes way beyond saying "I do." They are also submitting and coming under the authority of that young man's calling.

Whether we like it or not, Scripture defines our roles. The apostle Paul made it clear in I Corinthians 11:9 that "neither was the man created for the woman; but the woman for the man." This is God's plan, so you better make sure that you and Prince Charming carry the same burden, speak the same language regarding your future, and possess the same passions and desires. But on the other side, when you understand your role and place within the bounds of marriage, you do not see submission through the eyes of bondage or suppression but much the opposite. Great freedom is released in a woman's life and ministry when submission is active—a freedom that can come through no other source.

And, ladies, this is the bright side: You get to *choose* whom you submit to. If you get your life in a mess and begin to feel defeated in your calling because you married Fred, whom *you knew* had a burden for Indonesia, and now you can't stand the thought of leaving Mama and your church buddies to go to a foreign field, remember what you read in this book! When you say, "I do," the day you stand before God and man at the altar of marriage and commit your vows to one another, you are also submitting yourself in the sight of God to that young man's calling.

Think of what a powerhouse couple can accomplish for the kingdom of God when two like-minded, like-passioned, and equally yoked callings unite! Deuteronomy 32:30 talks about how one can put a thousand to flight, but two (who are united) can put ten thousand to flight. God can mightily use a couple who have the same vision and passion for His kingdom. The best advice I can possibly give to a single young woman who feels a call of God upon her life is to "marry up." What I mean by *marrying up* is to make sure you marry a young man you (right now) look up to and respect as far as his spiritual walk with God. Find a young man who is already grounded and rooted in a daily prayer life, demonstrates a godly lifestyle when no one is looking, and someone you can respect now. For a woman to have to rise and become the spiritual leader in her home and marriage is like climbing uphill with a backpack full of rocks—it will not be an easy road. While you are single, you have the privilege of choosing someone you can respect and honor all the days of your life, so make your choices built on prayer.

Understand what you are signing up for when you marry a young man who has a call of God upon his life because you will take on the responsibility of that call as well. As "two become one" you will also unite in calling and will carry the responsibilities that come with that call of God. I want to say again, there is something powerful about a couple who are sold out for the cause of the Kingdom! When both are united and have the same mind-set about ministry, they can become a powerful source God can work through to transform many lives and accelerate the Kingdom.

2 | *Activating the Call*

It seems like everywhere we turn, someone we know is fighting the hideous disease of cancer. People are afraid, and they are spending millions of dollars on vitamins and supplements, trying to clean their liver, purge their colon, and flush their kidneys. They take all kinds of antioxidants, trying to defend their bodies against cancer cells. All the while, they are ignoring and bypassing their largest and most important organ of all.

Wherever you are right now, I want you to stretch out your arm, pull up your sleeve, and touch your skin. Did you know your skin (or epidermis) is the largest and most important organ in your body?

Every day we lather our skin and feed it with lotions and deodorants that contain methylparaben, ethylparaben, and a family of "parabens" that have been linked not only to feeding cancer but to forming and creating cancer cells. Those who are taking all the internal supplements are wondering why they are still being attacked by cancer while never understanding the great importance their skin plays in the health of their entire body.

Now, before I lose you, this is not a lesson on health. Just like many sincere individuals have overlooked the largest and most important organ in their physical body, a woman who feels a call to ministry can easily overlook the number-one source of all ministries' birth: *An everyday, consistent prayer life.* A consistent prayer life is the rock behind the ministry God is calling you to. A consistent prayer life is the oxygen required in each breath of direction, anointing, and strength in the call of ministry. Everything you will ever become for the Kingdom will flow from your prayer life; even the calling itself will be birthed from your prayer life.

If you don't read another chapter in this book, please listen to what is being passed to you in the next few pages. A consistent, everyday prayer time that you set aside for just you and God is not only important, but it's essential. You cannot truly have any type of anointing or power without a prayer life because your prayer life nurtures relationship, and from that relationship the fountain of the Spirit is allowed to flow through you. Your prayer closet is the connecting point for this fountain to flow, and if it is forsaken or its importance is never really understood, the flow of power that comes from the fountain will dry up in a woman's life.

Claudette Walker confirms the fact that everything regarding ministry flows from her prayer closet. She never pursued a call to ministry but first sought a relationship with the Lord. And from that relationship and consistent prayer life came the calling. She states:

If you want the Lord to use you, do not pursue ministry but rather *pursue the Lord*. The priests under the Old Covenant were called to minister to the Lord. Would the calling be less for those of us under the New Covenant? People who are so lost in this worldly and demonic system are not in need of a gifted speaker or someone with great pulpit skills; people are in need of the power of God! If you spend your life seeking to know our Lord through His Word and through prayer and fasting, you will never have to try to build your ministry. I have found that as I have sought His face and His wisdom, people are drawn to listen because they sense and feel the Lord inside me, which has flowed from my prayer life.

I love to read books and learn from others, but nothing will ever take the place of your own prayer closet. My passion in life has been to *hear the voice of the Lord*. When you hear His voice, He will open the doors for you to speak His Word, and you will simply become the conduit for His Word to His people.

I remember the day the Lord taught me this lesson. We had ministered on the staff of Calvary Church in Cincinnati for twenty-three years. God had asked my husband and me to leave a church family we dearly loved for my husband to become the president of the Tupelo Children's Mansion. We were packing, saints were calling and crying, and we were crying. The Paslay family had been good to us, and they were like family to us.

In the middle of all the boxes and the trauma of leaving our church after twenty-three years, I had promised to speak at the Texas ladies retreat. I had notes spread all over my bed, but nothing was registering with me. I was dreading going to Texas. As

I sat down, I could see the bathroom sink from my bed, and at that moment the Lord spoke to me and asked, "What does the water faucet do to get the water to flow through it?" I thought and answered, "It stays connected to the water source and stays cleaned out so the water can flow purely through it." Then He asked me, "Does the faucet strain to get the water to flow?" My answer was, "No, of course not." Then He gave me a life-changing paradigm. Jesus said, "All you have to do is stay connected to Me through prayer and study of My Word. I am your source. Fasting unto me will keep you rid of all the fleshly debris that would hinder the flow of My Spirit." I then had a visual image of me with one hand extended to the throne of God, and the pure, life-changing water of His Spirit flowing through my other hand, which was extended to the audience.

God loves His people and always wants to feed them His Word. When I view myself as always staying connected to an endless supply flowing from the throne and have a burden in my heart for God's thirsty people, I never need to strain for Him to flow through me. To me the essence of ministry is hearing a word from the Lord and then sharing it under His anointing with His people, but it all starts in the prayer closet.

Your prayer life is your life source. As a minister or minister's wife (which by all means is also a minister) you will many times become a target for the enemy, and your *prayer life* will be what keeps you strong and encouraged in the Lord during these times. In your prayer closet you will learn to hear the voice of the Lord and develop a keen awareness of when He talks.

When you really get hold of the life-changing power that a consistent prayer life will bring, you understand that you cannot truly live without it, much less minister without it.

Joy Haney makes this statement about the power of a prayer life:

> The greatest thing you can do, whether as a minister's wife, a lady minister, or missionary, is to find a place where you can pray and talk to God, for you will need Him every day and sometimes more desperately than others. You need a place where you can shut yourself in, where it is just you and Jesus. This is as important as natural breathing, for prayer is spiritual breathing. There is no greater place to be than in His presence. You can tell Him all things, and He understands. Not only does He come, but He also gives a peace concerning the things that trouble your mind. He wraps you in the warmth of His love and lifts you into the realm of faith and glory.

If God has called you to ministry, let your first step toward that calling be built on the foundation of a consistent prayer life because everything involving your ministry will flow from that fountain. If you cannot shut yourself in with God every day and seek His face and spend time with Him in prayer, then don't expect to be very effective. But if you can connect to the power that comes through a daily prayer life, God will begin to show His approval of your calling outwardly. Matthew 6:6 confirms this:

> But thou, when thou prayest, enter into thy closet,
> and when thou hast shut the door, pray to thy Father
> which is in secret; and thy Father which seeth in
> secret shall reward thee openly. (Matthew 6:6)

Your prayer life will vindicate and validate your calling. The anointing that flows from your prayer closet will validate the call of God upon your life because through your intimate relationship with the Lord these things will be birthed. Anyone can be taught to give a sermon. Anyone can teach a Bible study. There are pulpit masters a dime a dozen in this nation who can move crowds to tears with emotionally stirring stories and charismatic personalities but are void of the true power of the anointing. If you have been around a minister who has a true anointing of God upon his or her life, you have witnessed the difference between those who move with anointing and others who move crowds with tools of personality and an assortment of emotionally stirring stories. The anointing releases the power of the supernatural. The anointing brings repentance and fear of God. The anointing ignites faith, which in turn births promises into being. The anointing brings people to their knees or turns their faces toward God in faith, and the only place that anointing comes through is your prayer closet! It flows from a relationship with the Lord.

Bobbye Wendell says this about a consecrated lifestyle that goes along with a calling:

> The most important thing a woman should reach
> for is the consecration of her own life, which

envelops a prayer life. Everything is available for her at that time, and before anything else is considered, her life should be centered on prayer and soulwinning. Don't say you're called to preach or minister if you haven't won a soul. Reach for all of the opportunities until God opens other doors. So many times I have wondered how in the world God could use me in the way He has, just a little girl from Oil City, Louisiana, but I was hungry for God. I would say another important thing for a young woman to do is to hunger after the things of God. Go for the deep things of God. There is a difference between just having an appetite and true hunger. An appetite is just a taste of this and that, but hunger eats whatever is available, is never satisfied, and reaches for more.

The Word of God will come alive to you when you mix your reading with prayer. Think about how God opened the understanding of His Word through great revelations of the end time to Daniel, and that happened when he was in prayer, seeking after God. God brought great revelation and understanding to Peter when he was upon the rooftop in prayer—getting alone with God. Streams of fresh thoughts will rush over your mind and spirit when you spend time with God in prayer every day.

Charles Spurgeon, the great revivalist who also trained hundreds of ministers throughout his life, made this powerful statement:

Most ministers who depend upon God's Spirit will tell you that their freshest and best thoughts are not those which were premeditated, but ideas

> which come to them, flying on the wings of angels;
> unexpected treasures brought on [*sic*] a sudden by
> celestial hands, seeds of the flowers of paradise,
> wafted from the mountains of myrrh.[1]

I remember hearing a message preached by our beloved Sister Nona Freeman. Nona Freeman and her husband, E. L. Freeman, were missionaries to Africa for many years and were both great people of faith who witnessed many miracles. Nona Freeman carried a great anointing upon her life when she ministered to the many crowds after they moved back to the United States. If you ever had the privilege of sitting under her ministry, you would agree to the great anointing that covered her when she ministered.

During this message, which was preached many years ago, she was addressing women in ministry or those who were married to ministers. She began to discuss the absolute necessity of having a consistent, everyday prayer life in order for God to use you effectively. She said when her children were young (she had five children), they took so much time and energy out of her during the day, plus trying to help her husband on the mission field, by the time she got the kids to bed she was so exhausted she was only able to give God her leftovers. The fact of not being able to spend time with the Lord began to weigh heavy upon her, but she didn't know what to do.

One night as she was talking to the Lord, He spoke to her these words, "You don't need all that sleep." Then He began to tell her to set her alarm clock for 2 AM and meet with Him in the early morning hours. He told her that if she would pursue Him in this way, He would make sure she never felt the void of that hour of sleep. Nona Freeman decided to trust God, and that night she set her alarm for 2 AM. When it went off, she crawled out of bed very quietly and found a room alone where she began to talk with the Lord. After she prayed an hour, she would go back to bed until around 7:00 AM, when she had to get the kids ready for school.

It made such a dramatic difference in her life and ministry that from that day forward she never looked back but made 2:00–3:00 AM her meeting time with God for the rest of her years.

She said that during those early morning hours, God would speak to her so clearly. During that hour of prayer, inspiration for messages and inspiration for books would begin to flow. It was as if she had a direct pipeline into the heavens, and God waited every morning to speak and give instruction to her. She learned the power of early-morning prayer!

THE POWER OF EARLY-MORNING PRAYER
(excerpts from *God Has a Waiting Room*)
I remember as a young twenty-year-old newlywed bride, my husband and I lived with his parents for about six months before we left to go evangelizing. I don't encourage this, but it made sense at the time to save money. We stayed in the nice, big bedroom that my husband's parents had built for him downstairs because he had made them believe he was never getting married.

I remember the first time I heard it. It was the early morning hours, and the sky was still dark outside when the sound of . . . oooo . . . (said in my best ghost howl) came through the vents from the upstairs bedroom. No, it wasn't a ghost, I so gladly found out, but it was the sound of my mother-in-law praying in the early morning hours. She would shut herself in the closet of one of the upstairs bedrooms every morning and pray. That planted something very deep inside me as I began to understand there are certain channels that God works through.

She had always told me, "Kim, if you want God to use you, you must develop an everyday, consistent prayer life. It's the most important thing you could ever do." As a young minister's wife, I tried to be consistent but so many times fell off the wagon more than I stayed on. It wasn't until around the second year of our marriage that my husband began to develop some major health issues, and the weight that came upon me in trying to figure out how to handle this pushed me to the prayer closet. I began to carry a cross in life, and during this time I began to uncover for myself not only the power but the extreme necessity of meeting with the Lord every day, it became my refuge.

In this place of early-morning prayer, I really began to know Jesus in a way I had never known Him before. You don't have to come to Him with big, fancy words or talk to Him in the King James Version; just talk to the Lord from your heart. Begin with worship and praise, then go into thanksgiving and remind Him of all the things you are thankful for. I always keep my Bible in my closet where I pray each morning, and many times I will just open it to the Book of Psalms and pray the prayers David lifted to the Lord. Become a little child in His presence and allow the tears to flow as He wraps you in His arms and just holds you close to Him. In this place of supplication praying, He heals you and strengthens you; here Jesus speaks peace to your spirit and fortifies it with faith when all hell is coming against you.

I want to uncover and set before you a treasure that, if taken seriously and applied to your life, will alter you so that you will never be the same. Our forefathers implanted certain spiritual secrets into their lives that made them successful in dealing with the spirit world. The Scriptures tell us to follow after these role models and to apply these patterns to our own lives.

> And we desire that every one of you do shew the same diligence to the full assurance of hope unto the end: that ye be not slothful, but followers of them who through faith and patience inherit the promises. (Hebrews 6:11–12)

My husband has always gotten up in the early morning hours and prayed, many times waking at 2:00 or 3:00 AM. He believes there is a more direct line of access to God in the early morning hours because the spirit world is not as stirred up then as later. Spirits are connected to people, and when people are not as active, spiritual activity is affected as well.

Now I understand this is not a very popular subject because the flesh hates rising early in the morning, and it's inconvenient to do so. How well I know this! Every morning I have to get myself out of bed as my body screams for that extra hour of sleep. From the very beginning, you and I were designed to commune with the Spirit of God in the early morning hours, and I'm going to endeavor to prove this.

Let's look at the lifestyle and patterns of the patriarchs who walked with God. Genesis 19:27 tells us Abraham had a specific *time* and specific *place* he met with God every day: "And Abraham gat up early in the morning to the place where he stood before the LORD."

Job offered sacrifices and burnt offerings for his children in the early morning hours. This would be the same as us praying over our children.

> And it was so, when the days of their feasting were gone about, that Job sent and sanctified them [his children], and rose up early in the morning, and offered burnt offerings according to the number of them all: for Job said, It may be that my sons have sinned, and cursed God in their hearts. Thus did Job continually. (Job 1:5)

David understood the power of early-morning prayer:

> My voice shalt thou hear in the morning, O LORD; in the morning will I direct my prayer unto thee, and will look up. (Psalm 5:3)

> O God, thou art my God; early will I seek thee: my soul thirsteth for thee, my flesh longeth for

thee in a dry and thirsty land, where no water is. (Psalm 63:1)

The most powerful example was Jesus Himself. As God manifest in flesh, Jesus showed us by His example there is something spiritually connected to early-morning prayer.

And in the morning, rising up a great while before day, he went out, and departed into a solitary place, and there prayed. (Mark 1:35)

A woman who has a call of God upon her life cannot afford to bypass a certain time and a certain place she meets with God every day. Something powerful takes place in early-morning prayer! An anointing will rest upon you and follow you throughout the day when you're willing to make the sacrifice to get up early to seek God. You will see your prayers answered and your faith rise to new levels when you put forth the effort to connect with God in the early morning hours.

There are pathways in the Spirit realm, and we can either take God's chosen pathway or we can choose to make our own way, which is many times more convenient to our lifestyles. If you want to live in the realm of the Spirit and walk in the anointing that was intended for you, you have to learn to flow in God's methods and channels. Isaiah 14:12 calls Lucifer the "son of the morning," or "son of the dawn" (NIV). He was, at one time, a high-ranking official in the courts of Heaven, and we know Lucifer lost his place because of his pride and was cast down to the earth and removed as the son of the morning. Even though he lost his position, he has not lost his nature. He knows the channels God operates through because he lived in the presence of God, and it is still in his heart to arrange things in our lives so that we become too busy to be able to tap into the power of early-morning prayer.

There was a reason God fed the children of Israel with manna from Heaven every morning. This shows us He has spiritual food for His people every morning, but if we don't understand this powerful insight and get up out of bed to receive this food, we are going to lose what God has provided for us to prepare us for the activities of the day. We will lose that time of visitation and bypass the anointing that is breathed upon us during those early morning hours.

A power will rest upon you and an anointing will follow you all day long when you tap into the source of early-morning prayer. You will be a woman who is led by the Spirit wherever you go—in the grocery store, the aisles of Wal-Mart, your place of employment—you will be in the flow of the Spirit that comes from connecting with what God has for you in your prayer closet!

THE SECRET TO A PRAYER LIFE

The main hindrance to our developing a prayer life is this: The flesh does not want to take the time to pray, and often we don't know how to pray. Even Jesus understood this when He asked His dedicated disciples to pray with Him for one hour. He found them sleeping and said, "Watch and pray, that ye enter not into temptation: the spirit indeed is willing, but the flesh is weak" (Matthew 26:41).

Claudette Walker talks about the responsibilities of (1) a prayer life, (2) Bible reading, and (3) feeding God's sheep.

I feel my greatest responsibility in ministry is to build a relationship with Jesus through prayer. I am a student of prayer. When I was a child at the Tupelo Children's Mansion, I loved to go for evening devotions to Aunt Stella's dorm because she knew how to touch God. I would kneel right next to her and listen more than I prayed. I am sixty-six years old today and still look for people who have a special anointing to pray, and I ask them to pray for me. I listen to them pray. I read books on prayer. And I learn to pray myself. The subject is extensive but its importance cannot be overstated. I want to hear someone preach who knows God, someone who knows His voice and has a deep and intimate walk with our Lord. I am still learning about prayer as I am growing in prayer and hungering to learn new ways to inter-act more deeply with the Lord. I feel it is the foundational call of any minister, male or female.

The second greatest responsibility to me is to have a passion for the written Word of God. In my daily Bible reading I try to read until something speaks to me. When I hear a word in my spirit while reading the Bible, I then stop and write what I learned. I always date the journal in the margin so that I can easily find the lessons by date. I also want to mention that I have *never* picked up the Bible looking for a message to preach. Every message God has given to me and I have spoken was birthed in my daily Bible study to *know the Author!* I believe that every message should be an overflow of your interaction with the Word in your quest to know God. People do not need a polished orator; they need Jesus! I look at my Bible as sixty-six love letters from my heavenly Bridegroom, for I remember no one had to talk me into reading the love letters my soon-to-be husband, Marvin, wrote to me when we were engaged. It was a joy! I would highlight his words to me and memorize the really good parts. With all my heart I encourage you to read the Word, study the Word, memorize the Word, and quote the Word! People are starving for an anointed word from the Lord.

I feel that my third responsibility is to feed God's sheep. Jesus asked Peter if he loved Him, and when Peter replied that he did indeed love the Lord, Jesus commanded him to feed His sheep. The entire purpose for ministry is to feed hungry people His Word and to give drinks of the living water of His Spirit to thirsty people. How that is accomplished is different in each of our lives, but the call is the same.

Our spirit, the inner person that hears the voice of God, is willing and desires to get alone with the Lord every day to seek after Him and to hear His voice, but the hindrance is our flesh. Our flesh does not want to pray. I'm sure that does not come as some great revelation to you because if you are made of flesh and blood, I'm sure you would agree if you were honest. Our flesh does not want to take the time to get out of bed an hour early, go into our closet or empty room, and talk to someone we cannot physically see. Our flesh does not like to put a halt in our busy schedule, find a dark prayer room, and get alone with God. I'm just being honest. It's not convenient to our lifestyles.

Paul, one of the greatest men of God who ever lived, confessed to wrestling with his flesh:

> For I know that in me (that is, in my flesh,) dwelleth no good thing: for to will is present with me; but how to perform that which is good I find not. For the good that I would I do not: but the evil which I would not, that I do. (Romans 7:18–19)

I don't know about you, but I'm so glad the Word of God just lays it out there and is transparent enough to let me know that it's normal to struggle with my flesh. It may be normal, and it may be something that you and I have to fight on a daily basis, but if we listen and obey that voice of self, if we go by what we feel, we will wind up on a road that we never had intentions of traveling. Paul understood this fight, but he also understood that it is a choice we have to make. It's a choice you make every day, and that choice directs your future and determines how you will be used of God.

> This I say then, Walk in the Spirit, and ye shall not fulfil the lust of the flesh. For the flesh lusteth against the Spirit, and the Spirit against the flesh: and these are contrary the one to the other: so that ye cannot do the things that ye would. (Galatians 5:16–17)

I believe another reason we don't desire to pray is because prayer has been presented as a duty, or we have this mentality that it's just another obligation we have to fulfill that day. And when we *do* make the time to get alone with God, we have such long lists of our own prayer needs plus another long list of needs we told other people we would pray about that the whole hour of prayer has become nothing more than God becoming our ATM machine when we're broke or just a Savior to a lost world. Don't get me wrong. He is our provider and our Savior, but when your prayer time is consumed with only bringing needs to God, we are missing the main purpose of prayer. Our hour of prayer becomes a job rather than what it was meant to become in our lives: building and nurturing a relationship with our Lord.

No wonder our flesh does not want to take the time to fit it into our schedule. Life is demanding enough and carries enough pressures on its own without having to add another job to our list. But I believe the Lord is going to give revelation and understanding to some sincere woman of God reading this. If we can get back to what a prayer life should be about, which is relationship, it will take us to the place where we long to be with Jesus. Revelation states it clearly:

> Thou art worthy, O Lord, to receive glory and honour and power: for thou hast created all things, and for thy pleasure they are and were created. (Revelation 4:11)

THE GREATEST COMMANDMENT
Jesus was teaching a group of religious leaders, Saddu-cees, who were considered the liberals of that day. They

didn't believe in the supernatural, they didn't believe in miracles, and they fought anything or anyone who taught these things. One of the scribes approached Jesus, and trying to catch Him in a trap, he asked Him, "Which is the first commandment of all?" Jesus looked at him, and without hesitation He said:

> The first of all the commandments is, Hear O Israel;
> The Lord our God is one Lord. (Mark 12:29)

This was the same commandment God told Moses to give to the children of Israel hundreds of years earlier in Deuteronomy 6:4. Jesus established that first and foremost you have to know that the Lord is one, and do not believe anything else anyone tries to tell you. Doctrine was established with Jesus' answer, but He was not finished.

> And thou shalt love the Lord thy God with all thy heart, and with all thy soul, and with all thy mind, and with all thy strength: this is the first commandment. (Mark 12:30)

So many people just stop at the fact there is one God, but Jesus said part two of the greatest commandment is to fall in love with that God. There is so much more to serving God than just believing in Him, having an experience at an altar, and going to church; Jesus wants His people to fall in love with Him. Your prayer time alone with God is where this will happen. Prayer is not just about interceding for souls, praying for revival, storming the gates of Hell, and praying for needs. While all of these are necessary, your prayer life should be centered first on learning how to fall in love with Jesus.

Remember how the Lord would come down in the cool of the day to walk and to talk with Adam and Eve in the garden? The great God of all glory, the Creator of the universe, wanted to have fellowship with His creation. He knew that making the choice to create humankind would eventually cost Him the pain and torture of Calvary, but His desire for love was so great that it was worth the cost to Him. I don't know about you, but when I think about this, it brings tears to my eyes. It makes me want to draw close to Jesus when I realize how much He wants to be near to me.

Sometimes Christians get so caught up in doing a "work" for God they don't realize they are bypassing the most important commandment. He wants us to love Him during our prayer time. He wants us to come to Him as that little three-year-old girl who crawls on the lap of her daddy and learns to love him and learns how to allow him to love her back. When you pray, it's all right to talk to God like a little child talks to her father; in fact, that is the relationship Jesus wants with us.

> For ye have not received the spirit of bondage again to fear; but ye have received the Spirit of adoption, whereby we cry, Abba, Father. The Spirit itself beareth witness with our spirit, that we are the children of God. (Romans 8:15–16)

What if you went to your earthly dad only when you were in trouble or you needed some money? Or, if you're married, what if you spent time with your husband only when you needed him to pay off your credit card? How do you think it would make them feel? We are made in the image of God, and the emotions, needs, hurts, and rejections that you and I go through, the Lord Jesus feels those same things when His children do not want to spend time with Him until they need Him to fix something. A normal child runs to the front door of the house when her dad comes home from work, throws her arms around his neck, and tells him she missed him. This is what Jesus wants from us when we make time for Him each day. We can never truly know Him or truly fall in love with Him until it is birthed in our time we spend with Him each day.

Altar experiences are wonderful when you're broken, weeping at the foot of the altar after a powerful word of the Lord has gone forth, but you cannot live off your altar experiences. Those will fade with time if they are not followed by a pursuit of God. A relationship of love is what will keep you through any storm or trial life brings your way. Your relationship with Jesus is what will keep those altar experiences hot and burning in your life. When you first pursue a relationship with Jesus, everything else in your ministry will begin to flow because it's flowing out of a relationship with your Father.

Another reason why the first and most important commandment was to love God is this fact: God *will not always answer your prayers the way you think they should be answered.* If you are serving God for the things He does for you or for the blessings He places upon your life, when He does not do exactly what you prayed for, it will cause tension in your relationship with Him. If you're not in love with Him, you will easily become offended and even become angry at God.

I cannot tell you how many times I have watched people sincerely pray for someone to be healed, and that person was not healed. That person praying has been me. Or they prayed God would open an opportunity for a promotion at work, and they were passed over and someone else got the job. I have watched people's attitudes change, although they would never admit it. We know God always can heal, deliver, or change a situation, but sometimes (in His perfect wisdom) He doesn't. But when you fall in love with Jesus, it doesn't matter what He does or does not do; you can handle it because your love for Him will birth a trust in His decisions.

Too many people love the church and never fall in love with the God of the church. Too many people (ministers included) have fallen in love with the safety and the fellowship of the church, or even the calling itself, but never come to the place they have really fallen in love with God. When storms rise and contrary winds begin to blow in their lives, they have no anchor to hold them because they haven't learned that it is a person's love for God that becomes her anchor when she goes through times of testing and questioning God's responses.

I remember counseling with a young woman a few years ago. She walked into my office, sat down, and completely blew me out of the water with something I was not expecting. She informed me she was done with serving God and was leaving the church. The reason this came as such a shock to me was because this woman was a prayer warrior. Every time Pastor called three days of prayer and fasting she was there, every prayer meeting she was present, and she knew how to pray. I would hear her in the church sanctuary on several occasions praying and interceding for revival.

I sat in complete awe. As she continued to talk, I silently prayed God would help me understand what was taking place and why this was happening. This was a situation in which I couldn't rely on counseling techniques or things I had used in the past—I needed distinct direction from the Holy Ghost. Suddenly, as she continued to talk, God spoke clearly to my spirit as He unfolded the reason behind all this: she never learned to fall in love with Jesus.

This woman was powerful in the Spirit, she knew how to cast out devils, she knew how to take spiritual authority and call out demonic oppression, but her relationship with the Lord was based on a "working" relationship, not a love relationship. She could quote Scripture and even operate in the gifts of the Spirit, but that alone was not enough to keep her when her world started falling apart. She never knew how to take off her battle garments and lay her sword down. Sadly, her prayer life became a battleground and nothing more. I tried to reach for her and talk to her about laying down her weapons and learning how to become a little child, but she had already made up her mind that she was done.

Thankfully, several years later, that woman made her way back to God, and to this day she is serving Him, but she is on a different level. Although she picked up a bunch of baggage during the years she strayed, she is now learning how to fall in love with Jesus and is building her relationship with Him upon the rock of relationship.

HOW TO PURSUE RELATIONSHIP

We have discussed the necessity of a prayer life and the priority of a prayer life. Now let's talk simply about how to begin or develop a prayer life.

A friend of mine had given me a copy of a message spoken at a meeting that was geared toward women being called to ministry, but it wasn't until a while later, while sitting on a plane, I decided to listen to this teaching. As I listened to it, much of it logical and sensible things a woman needs to know when feeling a call, my heart began to ache within me. I kept waiting for it to come. Not one word was mentioned about the importance of developing a prayer life. Nothing. Throughout the entire session there was not one time I heard anything mentioned about seeking after the Lord on a daily basis. It saddened me. I walked off that plane with a heavy heart but also with a renewed passion to declare to this generation the importance of prayer.

Anyone who has ever made a difference in the kingdom of God had a dedicated prayer life, for he or she understood this is where the fountain of the anointing flows. Leonard Ravenhill, who was a powerful evangelist in England and the US, made this statement about the prayer closet:

> The Cinderella of the church of today is the prayer meeting. This handmaid of the Lord is unloved and unwooed because she is not dripping with the pearls of intellectualism, nor glamorous with the silks of philosophy; neither is she enchanting with the tiara of psychology. She wears the homespuns of sincerity and humility and so is not afraid to kneel! . . .
>
> One does not need to be spiritual to preach, that is, to make and deliver sermons of homiletical perfection and exegetical exactitude. By a combination of memory, knowledge, ambition, personality, plus well-lined bookshelves, self-confidence, and a sense of having arrived—the pulpit is yours almost anywhere these days. Preaching of the type mentioned affects men; prayer affects God. Preaching affects time; prayer affects eternity. The pulpit can be a shopwindow to display our talents; the closet speaks death to display. Ministers who do not spend two hours a day in prayer are not worth a dime a dozen, degrees or no degrees.[2]

Woman of God, there is nothing more important than your having a prayer life!

Joy Haney discusses the practice of prayer:

> As a young minister's wife with young children, sometimes I felt torn between meeting the many needs of

my children, the housework, the work of ministry, and just life itself. As you hear the older women talk about secret places of prayer, daily prayer, and getting alone with God, you sometimes feel guilty because you cannot have this perfect schedule, and you end up feeling frazzled and frustrated.

If you truly want to develop a consistent walk with God even in the midst of potty training, nursing feverish brows, and fixing school lunches, I want to take the guilt from you. There are two ways to do this. We are told in the Bible to pray without ceasing, pray continually, and always to pray. I had a fervent desire for the things of God. I had been raised in a home that put much emphasis on prayer and had seen it demonstrated in our home, so it was a natural thing for me to want to continue in a practice that seemed to bring so much power and blessing.

I remember getting my two older children off to school, then taking care of my two younger ones by dressing and feeding them. I would take them down to the playroom, and there I would kneel and pray. Many were the times they would play "horsey" on my back, and say, "Mommy cry." I would hug and kiss them and say, "Mommy is talking to Jesus."

When my children grew older, my secret place of prayer was in the morning before they awakened. This was not difficult for me because I had been raised to get up at 6:00 AM every morning while growing up as a child. During that time of the morning everything was quiet and still and there were no phones ringing, no one knocking at the door, just peace with God before the day began. No task, person, or thing should be allowed to take away the relationship you have with Jesus.

Whether we want to admit to it or not, we do what we want to do. Whatever is truly important to us, we will make it fit in our schedule. If you found out that your favorite department store was having every item in the store 75 percent off for one day, you better believe you would make time in your day to hit that sale! When we understand and realize how important our prayer lives are, nothing on our schedules has the power to take it from us. We do what we want to do. That's it. If we want to connect to the One who loves us and desires to speak to us, strengthen us, and comfort us, we will make the time in our busy schedules to meet with Jesus. As a minister's wife for over twenty-five years, I don't know how I would have made it through some of the storms that have come my way if I didn't have a prayer life. I can honestly say it's been the only thing that kept me afloat when everything seemed broken in my life.

I have wonderful saints in my church who tell me, "Sister Haney, I'm praying for you." I thank God for everyone who prays for me, but I know I cannot live on their prayers. No one can take the place of Kim Haney praying for herself. I honestly don't know of anyone who can pray for Kim Haney more powerfully or with greater burden than myself. I know my weaknesses, and my prayer closet becomes a safe place where I can expose them. Here I can repent and ask God to cleanse me if I have talked about someone or when pride or bitterness starts knocking at the door of my heart. No one else but God and I know the times I am dealing with some major heart issues, and if I don't drink from the fountain of supplication and examine my heart before God, expose, and release things that nobody else knows I'm dealing with on a daily basis, these diseases will eventually take over my life.

So many people (ministry included) have the mentality that a prayer life is all about praying for Sister Suzie's aunt's daughter who has a sore throat. Or Brother James's uncle who can't get his car to start. Don't tell me I'm the only one alive who has those types of requests now and then. People are people anywhere you live.

We, as ministry, must understand that, first of all, we have to pray over our own lives. We have to cover our own souls with prayer because the enemy would like nothing more than to invade our territory and rob us of our intimacy with God. He would love for our prayer times to become "clocking in and clocking out" and become a "because I know I need to" business relationship. The enemy tries to make us feel guilty if we are not constantly praying for revival or for the needs of our saints or constantly in warfare against the powers of darkness. Trust me, there is a place and a time for that. But when those things on the outside begin to wholly consume our time alone with the Lord, and we don't have time to seek relationship, it will eventually rob us of our faith in God, it will steal the joy we are intended to walk in, and we will become weak, exhausted, weary women of God who become frustrated and irritated with everyone around us. According to Nehemiah 8:10, the joy of the Lord gives us strength. But notice where that joy comes from. According to Psalm 16:11, the fullness of joy comes from *His presence*.

It's not enough to have a relationship with the building or the leader; if you don't have a relationship with God, you're going to be in trouble. It's impossible to lead others if you do not have a relationship with God, because you can only give out of what you first possess personally. God is teaching His people how to approach Him, how to get into His presence and into the Holy Place where the shekinah glory hovered and the miraculous was manifested. That's the glory that comes through a prayer life.

3 | *You Are Enough for the Call*

I will never forget the feeling of extreme unworthiness as long as I live.

It was the year 2001, and many rumors had been circulating regarding my dear father-in-law being voted in as the general superintendent of the United Pentecostal Church International. As a family, we had all been praying God's perfect will, whatever that may be, knowing there would be great change that would follow if God opened the door for this position. The ballots were cast as we sat high in the middle section of the arena bleachers, holding our breath. As the results came in, stating the fact Kenneth Haney had been voted into this honorable position, we felt great excitement mixed with uncertainty. I never realized the incredible weight of responsibility that would soon be laid upon my shoulders.

That afternoon several of the family and extended family members, which consisted of many pastors and ministers of various types, all met in a small room to discuss the transition and to pray a covering over whatever the next season had in store. We laid our hands upon my mother- and father-in-law, asking God's special anointing to rest upon them for this endeavor they were undertaking, and then came our turn. As my husband and I stepped forward and the ministry laid their hands upon us to "pass the torch," so-to-speak, it was as if a blindfold had been removed from my eyes. At that moment, the unveiling of the great pressure and responsibility I was undertaking became touchable. Why is it that life has its way of taking us from one uncomfortable place to another? This step was no longer something in the future that seemed far away, but I was living it. As the tears streamed down my face, I was also aware of the new face of fear that had slipped beside me in this vulnerable time.

I cried because I was scared about the future. I cried because I felt so unworthy and unqualified to step into the shoes of Joy Haney, Olive Haney, and the great women who had gone before them. I even thought maybe God had made a mistake in His decision, but now there was no way out. But also that day someone else stepped into that room as the feeling of absolute unworthiness wrapped its hands around my throat and tried to choke the life out of me. That fear whispered its lies that, yes, to be completely transparent, a certain part of me wanted to believe. I knew the steps of a good man were ordered of the Lord, I knew all the clichés that people tell you and all the fancy Scriptures they twist trying to make you feel better, but they weren't standing in my shoes. They weren't the one having to go back to Christian Life Center in Stockton, California, to face thousands of people and gain their acceptance as the new pastor's wife while the whole world looked on.

Between the two churches God had called my husband and I to start and the couple of years of evangelizing, we had been involved with Christian Life Center for several years here and there, but now I was facing this world in a new way that overwhelmed me. That spirit of unworthiness had now turned into the face of fear as it tried to control me through the way I thought of myself. *But that was not the way God saw me.* That is the key. I can look back on those days and see it now, but I didn't understand it then. Satan will attack us through our minds and the things we *allow* ourselves to dwell on, and if we are not careful, they may become spiritual strongholds in our lives.

The difficult part in recognizing these strongholds is that, most of the time, the lies the enemy feeds us are mixed with the sugar of logic. They make sense. We internalize these thoughts about ourselves, how unworthy we are, our lack of talents and abilities, and then allow the outgrowth of those thoughts to distort our thinking and eventually determine who we become. Satan will fight with all of his clever and cunning schemes a woman who has a call of God upon her life. He knows how powerfully you can be used in the kingdom of God, and if he can get you to accept his lies, he is able to control you, your effectiveness, and most importantly, the people of God.

From the book, *Christians and Strongholds,* I want to reemphasize how the enemy works in our minds:

> Satan brings these deceptive thoughts into people's minds and then persuades them to accept those ideas about themselves, the way others see them, the (false) way God sees them, or the way life is destined to turn out for them. When we allow these thoughts to roam free and are not aware of what is happening, we begin to accept them as ours, and the stronghold's construction begins as the enemy sits back and laughs.
>
> Block upon block, stone upon stone, the walls are allowed to be built internally, and we do not recognize what is happening. We do exactly what we were warned not to do and become ignorant of Satan's devices and accept these thoughts as our own.[3]

I saw myself as unworthy. I saw myself as unfit. I saw myself as unable and incapable. If I had continued on that road carried by my own thoughts that the enemy was using against me, who knows where I would be today? I cannot tell you that I had a visitation from an angel or some supernatural confirmation to let me know that God thought I was enough. I never can remember anyone speaking into my life other than one occasion when God used Claudette Walker (whom I did not even know at the time) to prophesy to me during a Ladies' Landmark meeting. Nobody knew I was going through this attack, but God knew, and He sent precious Claudette Walker onto the scene to speak into my life a word from the Lord to expose exactly what I was being taunted and tormented with.

From that day forward something began to change inside of me. The change did not happen overnight because the enemy doesn't want to let go of anyone that easily, but I can tell you with sincere honesty that the secret of overcoming my extreme insecurity and unworthiness was the fact that I learned to pray and develop a daily prayer life. That was the answer. Years before this transition took place I had learned the power of an early-morning prayer life, and through this channel God began to change who I thought I was into what He wanted me to be for His kingdom. Through my personal and intimate relationship with Jesus every morning, pouring out my heart and insecurities to Him, Jesus began to pour a new mold inside me. The best way to explain it is exactly what happened to Saul when He was chosen by God to become Israel's first king.

Here was Saul, just a young man who was out looking for his father's donkeys when the prophet Samuel came into his life sent by God. God chose Saul even though he never went searching or pursuing after any kind of position. He was God's chosen vessel. God will pick and choose the most random people to fulfill the needs of His kingdom. Saul was nobody special; he had no prerequisites or abilities that made him eligible for the position God was calling him to. His insecurity was evident when he turned to Samuel and explained his position in the community:

> And Saul answered and said, Am I not a Benjamite, of the smallest of the tribes of Israel, and my family the least of all the families of the tribe of Benjamin? Why then do you speak like this to me? (I Samuel 9:21, NKJV)

After Samuel poured anointing oil over Saul's head, the Bible says the Lord gave Saul "another heart."

> So it was, when he had turned his back to go from Samuel, that God gave him another heart; and all those signs came to pass that day. (I Samuel 10:9, NKJV)

In Hebrew this expression literally reads, "God changed him for another heart." This was a work of God's Spirit that prepared Saul in a supernatural way for the calling that was upon his life. It no longer was the old Saul who stepped into the position that was required of him, but God put something supernatural inside him that was beyond his natural abilities and helped him fulfill what the call required. Saul had never prophesied or operated in the realm of the Spirit, but when this "new heart" was placed inside him, we see him prophesying with the group of prophets that met him in the next verse. We know that Saul started out meek, humble, and obedient to the Lord, but as time went by, he made some choices and decisions that were pressed by the root of pride. Instead of being willing to confront this attack, keep his spirit under subjection, and turn to God with repentance and humility, Saul allowed that spirit of pride to control him, and it eventually became his destruction.

Through prayer and pouring my soul out to the Lord, the way I thought about myself began to change, and my insecurities were no longer able to control me. I began to find myself in Him and not how I saw myself, or how I perceived other people saw me. Something strange happened one day that gave me a wake-up call regarding my insecurity as the Lord exposed the mask it was hiding behind, the mask of pride. Insecurity and unworthiness are a false humility that stems from the root of pride. Worrying about not living up to other people's expectations, concern over failing or not being perfect, unwillingness to accept yourself, trying to be more like someone else, obsession with what others think of you—all of these feelings and emotions are damaging because they come with the purpose of destroying the will of God for our lives.

Trust me, you will fail at times. You will not always be perfect or able to please everyone. Not everyone will always like you or want to be your friend. You will not always be supported or understood, but if you become a woman of prayer, fight every day to keep your heart right and your spirit pure, and learn to hear the voice of God and cultivate a spirit of humility. Your days of support, love, and encouragement will be many more than the days of the opposite.

Joy Haney says this about the power of your mind:

> Your heart, mind, and thoughts are all centered in your brain, and your brain controls your body. You cannot do anything without first receiving a message from the brain. The mind is a mass of thoughts, memories, feelings, and emotions. Emerson said, "You are what you think about all day long." No matter what your external appearance, the real you is hidden in your heart, which is connected to your mind.
>
> First Peter 1:13 says, "Wherefore gird up the loins of your mind." This means to use actions in

cleansing out the portions of our mind that produces thoughts. We must watch the thoughts that are allowed to linger in our minds, for they have the power to reproduce themselves and grow into giants that are hard to get rid of. If doubt, fear, and discouragement are not destroyed in the early stages, they will multiply and produce more thoughts of the same nature. We have to be aware of what kind of thoughts we are producing and allowing to live in our minds.

True humility is about having faith in God. It bypasses who you think you are or who you think you're not but places complete trust and confidence in God. All He asks for is complete, surrendered, sold-out vessels that are willing to be used! It's not about thinking highly of yourself, but it's about dying to your image and concern about what others may think of you, and hiding behind the Cross. Let the world see only the Cross as God begins to use you. Be His hands to someone who needs to feel His love, be His heart when you reach out to someone who is hurting, be His mouthpiece when the time comes to stand for righteousness. God will use those He can trust to lay aside their lack of qualifications and step out in faith as a willing vessel to be used for His glory!

Elsy Cunningham shares how God encouraged her when she felt unworthy of the call:

> As a young girl, I did not know that I would one day be involved in ministry. I always loved the work of God and was faithful to the things of God. My Apostolic heritage is very rich; in fact, the revival

in Colombia started on my paternal grandfather's plantation. My parents helped the missionaries but were not pastors themselves and were not considered to be ministers. My grandmother prayed for a Spanish church that preached the truth to be started in New York City. Oliver Spencer, who was living in the Midwest, saw my grandmother in a vision, and the Lord told him to go to New York City and start a Spanish church. He obeyed the voice of the Lord, and this is the church that I attended when I came to the United States.

My family was very involved in the church. Whatever needed to be done, we were there, desiring to serve in every area. No task was exempt, whether it was cleaning, remodeling, prayer vigils, or other activities; every job was accepted with humility and gladness. I was always excited about being in the church, and my mother was responsible for cultivating this characteristic in my life.

I never felt that I was worthy to be a minister's wife. Most of the ministers whom I was acquainted with said that my sister would be the one who would probably marry a minister, as she seemed to have all of the qualities of the stereotypical minister's wife. Later, in my teenage years, John Hopkins became my pastor. He, along with my grandmother and mother, told me that I had a heart for the things of God as I would study the Word of God for hours and spend time in prayer with my grandmother. Still, I did not think that I could be in ministry because I observed other ministers' wives and never thought I could fit the mold.

The defining moment came for me when I became Jack Cunningham's girlfriend. I told him that I would not fit into ministry. His response was, "What do you mean?" I gave him all of the reasons—I wasn't raised in a minister's home, I didn't think I was worthy, I didn't play music, and I was not an accomplished singer. He responded to me with encouragement and told me due to the fact that I loved people and had a servant's heart, those were the most important attributes that God was searching for.

We see them at ladies conferences, church services, banquets, meetings, anywhere the spotlight of the public eye can shine upon their lives. Women who minister into our lives through a preached word, an anointed Bible study, a powerful song, behind the scenes teaching a classroom full of Sunday school kids, leading a choir, sharing a testimony, wrapping their arms around a backslider who has come home, praying restoration for people in the altar, the list can go on and on. Who are these women whom God uses? Are they chosen by Him because they have a great Pentecostal pedigree or an impressive doctorate degree behind their names? Are they chosen by God because they have extreme talent and unlimited abilities? Does God call their names because they have incredible personalities and can sing like an angel? Absolutely not. God chooses His vessels according to the heart. When God chose David, He told Samuel what was important:

> But the LORD said unto Samuel, Look not on his countenance, or on the height of his stature; because I have refused him: for the LORD seeth not as man seeth; for man looketh on the outward appearance, but the LORD looketh on the heart. (I Samuel 16:7)

Throughout Scripture, God has given us insight on how He chooses His ministers. When the Lord went searching the earth to find a man whom He could pass His covenant promises to, He found a man by the name of Abraham. Passing by that day on His way to destroy the cities of Sodom and Gomorrah, He chose this man to carry His truth based on this powerful fact:

> And the LORD said, Shall I hide from Abraham that thing which I do; seeing that Abraham shall surely become a great and mighty nation, and all the nations of the earth shall be blessed in him? For I know him, *that he will command his children and his household after him,* and they shall keep the way of the LORD, to do justice and judgment; that the LORD may bring upon Abraham that which he hath spoken of him. (Genesis 18:17–19, emphasis mine)

The Lord based His choice of calling Abraham upon this one powerful statement: First, He *knew Abraham,* which tells us Abraham had a relationship with the Lord. Second, Abraham would understand the importance of not only himself becoming all-consumed, but he would pass a passion for a relationship with this God to his children. He wouldn't just pray with them or take them with him when he offered sacrifices, but he would teach his children and make sure the love for this truth was grounded and rooted deeply in them. Abraham taught his children to be serious when it came to the worship of their God so they, too, would be carriers of truth to their generation.

Now I understand this is not a book on parenting, but we do have to understand this was so important to God that it was the main basis He chose Abraham to carry forth His work. Not his family legacy. Not his wealth, though Abraham was wealthy. Not his ability to speak to the nations. Not even the fact that he had great faith. God knew Abraham would be loyal to the truth, he would not listen to any compromising spirits or voices, and he would pass on a love for truth to his children.

Paul wrote of the type of people God will call to do His work:

> For ye see your calling, brethren, how that not many wise men after the flesh, not many mighty, not many noble, are called: but God hath chosen the foolish things of the world to confound the wise; and God hath chosen the weak things of the world to confound the things which are mighty; and base things of the world, and things which are despised, hath God chosen, yea, and things which are not, to bring to nought things that are. (I Corinthians 1:26–28)

The *Benson Commentary* states that the people who God called

> were chiefly a few poor fishermen, of low parentage, of no learning or eloquence, of no reputation or authority, despised as Jews by the rest of mankind, and by the Jews as the meanest and worst of themselves. What improper instruments were these to contend with the prejudices of the world, the superstition of the people, the interests of the priests, the vanity of the philosophers, the pride of the rulers, the malice of the Jews, the learning of the Greeks, and the power of Rome!

In God's way of thinking, it was the weaker instruments who would be chosen to confound the things which are mighty. God will choose those who will best serve the purpose of His glory, and most of the time it will not be those who hold great power in the eyes of the world. The next verse explains why:

> That no flesh should glory in his presence.
> (I Corinthians 1:29)

FIRST REQUIREMENT FOR THE CALL: YOU MUST ACCEPT YOURSELF

Beyond the walls of unworthiness lies another blockade we must overcome: Learn to accept yourself and be content with your calling. Know that God has plans for you and accept that place in His kingdom. I'm not going to lie to you. Sometimes trying to *hear* the voice of God and *decide* where God wants you at the time and season you are presently in is the greatest challenge, but it may be a greater challenge to simply accept yourself and not try to become someone else or live in someone else's calling. It's something that is easier said than done.

Even back in the days of the apostles, they struggled to be secure in their specific talents and giftings without falling into the trap of comparing themselves among others who were used in the kingdom of God. Paul tried to address this:

> But as God hath distributed to every man, as the
> Lord hath called every one, so let him walk. And so
> ordain I in all churches. (I Corinthians 7:17)

Each called-of-God individual is born with certain traits and characteristics inside her DNA that
God has specifically designed for the lot in life she is
supposed to fill, and He doesn't want her to try to be
like someone else. The world tells us we need to try
to be someone else through subliminal messages in
media and advertisements. If you will look a certain
way, buy a certain car, drink this type of soda, wear
certain types of clothing, you will be accepted. This
spirit has also slipped into the church. With the influx
of social media, the spirit of competition rises inside
God's people to try to be something they are not or
fill a place that is not in the plan of God for them.

God told Jeremiah that even in his mother's womb He
knew him and He was shaping who he would become.

> Before I formed thee in the belly I knew thee; and
> before thou camest forth out of the womb I sanc-
> tified thee, and I ordained thee a prophet unto the
> nations. (Jeremiah 1:5)

When Paul addressed the subject of "walking in the
calling that God has distributed" he was basically saying
that God wants you to be who He created you to be.
He wants you to be the woman He formed in your
mother's womb and for you to use the talents, gifts,
and abilities as tools in your hand to give back to the
Kingdom. Too many people lose their identities and
try to become somebody else and fulfill someone else's

calling, which is not only impossible, but at the same time causes them to abort their own ministry.

This is not referring to times you have looked up to someone who has a powerful ministry or someone whom God has used and they have allowed themselves to be vessels in His hand. You need people of influence in your life, but we are talking about trying so hard to be like that person that you lose your own identity. It's a difficult thing when you're young and trying to find yourself and where you fit in the kingdom of God, but at the same time, stay under the influence of an older woman who has fulfilled her purpose and is reaping the results of what has taken years to accomplish.

I remember a young man in Bible college who absolutely admired and loved one of our powerful ministers in the movement. His admiration went beyond just allowing his life to become influenced by this man, but he became consumed with him. He would listen to his messages by the hours until he was able to mimic his voice perfectly and had memorized every cliché and phrase used by this minister. It even came to the place he began to walk like him, and I started to notice how other students began to laugh at him behind his back. This young man was talented in his own right, but he never came to the place of accepting his own identity and never became secure in who God had destined him to become.

It does not matter how much you love and adore a man or woman of God, how much you listen to his messages or study her mannerisms, you were never meant to be like him or her. God told Joshua that just as He was with Moses He would also be with him, but Joshua was never meant to become Moses. God wanted to use Joshua as himself. If a woman (of any age) does not come to this important understanding, she will live in frustration and a world of jealousy. She will never be content with her lot in life because God never intended for her to become another individual.

Donna Linville shares this powerful truth on not only recognizing but also *accepting* who God has called you to be:

> The greatest lesson I ever received, and one of the biggest altars I have ever built, was at a Ladies' Landmark meeting in Stockton, California. It was several years ago, and I had been asked to speak to the church that Sunday morning after the meeting. I had never even seen that magnitude of people except during a General Conference, as I stepped to that pulpit. There was Brother Kenneth Haney and his whole pastoral and college staff, who were great men with theology degrees, sitting behind me, and I was so fearful. Right at that time of great insecurity, God gave me enlightenment and told me one of the greatest altars I could ever build was the altar of limitations. Let me explain what I mean by the altar of limitations. If you are feeling a call to the ministry and you attend some meeting or another church and find yourself becoming resentful toward those who have growth, those who have a nice building, or even those whom God uses in ministry and places an anointing upon their lives, it's time to build an altar of limitation.
>
> If you're sitting there and looking at the magnitude that surrounds you, and you have never

built an altar of your limitations (and I'm not being negative), you will find yourself struggling with much greater enemies such as bitterness and jealousy. During this time, God showed me I had to build an "altar of limitations" to Him because back home we were just struggling to get a few people to come to church. The Lord spoke to me that day the parable that He told His disciples in Matthew 25 regarding what you do with the talents God gives to *you:* One talent, five talent, and ten talents. You have to build an altar to your limitations.

The servant who took his one talent and buried it because he didn't think it was enough or he resented those who had five and ten talents, God called him *wicked*. Right there, I built that altar to the Lord, and that was over twenty-five years ago. I released to God and to myself the fact that I am limited. I don't have any great administrative skills. Neither does my husband. We would not be able to control or pastor a church with a huge amount of people. I had to acknowledge and release that to God and say, yes, we have limitations. It does not mean you cannot learn to fix certain limitations, but it had nothing to do with my spirituality. It had nothing to do with my heart or my ministry God had called me to.

I have seen dynamic and spiritual pastors who pastor twenty people. They are spiritual and have a great calling upon their life, but they understood somewhere, you have to build an altar of limitations, or resentment can grow. The reason I am addressing this is because when you come to the place where you can acknowledge this fact, you will eliminate jealousy and envy! When you recognize your place in God's kingdom and understand there will be limitations, it releases you to grow in your own ministry, and then as you grow your ministry, God multiplies it. The altar of limitations was one of the biggest altars I have ever had to build in my life. I used to worry about how my husband and I would ever accomplish something big until the Lord spoke to me and said, "Limitations of talent." When He said that, it released me and gave me such peace.

There is liberating peace that comes into your life when you not only understand but you also *accept* the direction God has spoken to you for your life and purpose. The apostle Paul was clear when he addressed this very issue to those in the church of Corinth.

> Now there are diversities of gifts, but the same Spirit. And there are differences of administrations, but the same Lord. And there are diversities of operations, but it is the same God which worketh all in all. (I Corinthians 12:4–6)

In other words, people will operate and minister within the body of Christ in various ways. Different ministries will be released among the church, and the church becomes strong when those who are called are steadfast and accept what God has chosen for them.

When a generation steps off the scene, it can be one of the most fearful times for the church because the elders who pass on have left a spiritual establishment that is strong. If the younger generation does not go through their share of trials, storms, and tribulations, or if they have not responded to God properly through accepting their identity, there will be a giant deficit in spiritual power and trust in God. Israel went through this very thing. There were times the elders would pass on and go to their reward, and those who were behind them did not have the same commitment, lifestyle, passions, or hunger. This negatively affected God's people as a whole in a huge way.

Even though we are all equal in God's eyes, each generation still has to pay the price for the anointing and visitations of the Spirit, or it would not be fair to the generations who have gone on before. Every effective minister of God had to come to the place where he understood and accepted his unique gifting and callings. They all knew each member of the body of Christ had a particular function that was unique and designed especially for him or her to operate through.

> Now ye are the body of Christ, and members in particular. (I Corinthians 12:27)

Paul said we are "members in particular." God has placed the DNA inside each of us to be designed to function exactly where He places us. Society and even our flesh will try to convince us that whatever talents, gifts, and personality traits we were born with are inadequate for the work that God has set before us, trying to rob us of our confidence in the call of God upon our lives. They make us to think that we have to work toward becoming something we cannot be or someone else we were not meant to be in order to have value. The real issue behind that lie is while you are trying to become someone else, that lie will become the molder and controller of your future.

Bobbye Wendell discusses the subject of becoming confident in your calling:

> I would like to say something to the young women today: you are not *really* limited except for the limitations you put on yourself. There are better opportunities today and more freedoms for you to minister through. There are many areas of service available for you, and knowing this, it's important that you be instant in season and out of season. When God gives you an opportunity, you must walk through the doors, and God will honor all that you put yourself into.
>
> When we felt the call to Ethiopia, I could hardly wait to get there, but before we left, person after person came to us and said it could not be done. They made us to think we were wasting our time and it could not happen, but it did. I say to you: persevere and consecrate. You cannot run with the pack and truly be what God has called you to be. You have to separate and consecrate yourself and go deep with Him. When you think you've gone deep, go deeper. There is a constant call for us to go deeper.
>
> There is much more education among the women today than there was when I was hearing my call. Education cannot become your master, but you can make it your servant. It should never become what you depend upon, for your dependence should be the anointing. Education, a degree, or a license can never replace it. Persecution is coming to this country, and education will not fight it. Only the anointing will keep you strong, for we are dealing with a demon-possessed inheritance.

In America today we are dealing with every demonic spirit that ever filled a human being. There is only one thing that will control those dark elements of evil, the power of the name of Jesus used with the anointing God puts upon our lives.

My son asked me, "Mom, have you ever been mad at God about some of the things you've had to go through?" I turned to him and said, "No. I have never been mad at God, and I will never be mad at God." We have gone through some horrible things as a family, and I have never asked God why. To me, it's trust. I reminded my son about the early church people who were fed to lions and sawed in half; they didn't do anything wrong and they suffered. Just because you serve God does not mean you're going to sit on satin pillows the rest of your life. I know the visitation of pain and suffering and there will be times you will suffer, but we need strong workers. We need people who can dig out and dig down and offer themselves to God no matter what life brings their way.

Some of the most miserable people in the world are those who have never learned how to embrace, accept, and love themselves the way God intended for them to be. My friend, you are a specially designed vessel that God has carefully and uniquely planned out before you were ever born.

I remember as a young minister's wife, being blessed to have the influence of my mother-in-law, Joy Haney, in my life but at the same time feeling the unvoiced pressure that I had to be like her in order to be accepted. She played a huge role in my life; she taught me the value of a consistent prayer life, how to walk in the Spirit, and how to become a woman of faith—but God never intended for Kim Haney to be Joy Haney. Joy Haney was never meant to become Olive Haney, who was her pastor's wife.

You glean certain traits and catch things that can be passed to you in the Spirit from great men and women of God who influence you and form who you become. This is why you need the influence of godly elders. Nothing can replace what a godly elder can pass to you spiritually. I remember the struggle that I went through for several years, never believing I could measure up to the "perfect pastor's wife," and the pressure I was feeling was mostly created by me. I began to think that in order to be a successful minister's wife my personality had to change, my interaction with others had to be altered, and I was supposed to respond to things and react to people the exact way I had watched others respond.

I cannot tell you the exact day that it happened, but as I began to pray and draw close to the Lord, He revealed to me that my personal identity was given to me for a reason. If I were going to be anything usable for God's service, I would have to accept the fact that I was not intended to be anyone else. My friend, I cannot tell you how liberating that was for me, understanding that everything I needed for my specific calling and for my generation was built inside of me by God! And *in God's timing* those doors would open. I learned that God not only wanted me to become the personality He made me, but also that this damaging mentality I had would limit Him from being able to use me the way He desired.

If God wanted a certain person to be born and minister in your place for your generation, He is powerful enough to have placed that person in your stead. You are not born in this generation by accident. God has strategically set you in place, with your certain gifts, personality, disposition, and nature, to be effective to the people in your world. Stand up with Holy Ghost boldness, for if God has chosen you, He will use you! Your own mentality and negative image of yourself will be your greatest enemy, and only you have the power to hold yourself back with lame excuses as to why you're not good enough, smart enough, or talented enough. You can feel as if everyone is against you, you're too old, too young, never went to Bible college, the list can go on and on for miles. We blame too many things on the devil when he hasn't even been involved in any of it because all he has to do is sit back and smile as he watches you destroy your own calling through your distorted mentality. Get yourself out of the lame "me" mentality, which hides under the mask of pride and pity, and put your best foot forward, as a willing vessel, to do whatever God has placed before you.

Joy Haney makes this statement about accepting yourself:

> Sometimes women of today feel that they are not important if their name is not flashing in lights for all the world to see and admire. In a very subtle way, humanism emphasizes the physical person to the point of obsession while downplaying the

inner person. Women are made to feel guilty if they do not weigh 110 pounds, have peaches-and-cream skin, and have bodies that sway, bend, and look fabulous. Americans have come to the point of body worship whereas the Bible puts emphasis on the whole person: physical, social, spiritual, and mental. When God called a woman great in the Old Testament, it was not because of how she looked but because of what she *was and did*.

I have a dear friend who is an incredible example of a woman who has given God her all, no matter what season life has thrown her way. With every change that has come into her life, which she had no control over, she has looked for the needs instead of burying herself in her own pity. Donna Hogue has been my right-hand helper in Women's Ministry for over twenty years, and before that she was a helper to my mother-in-law. She has been effective in ministering to thousands of women through the years and is the true definition of a woman who has been effective in ministry.

Donna Hogue shares her story of how you can be enough for every season of life that comes your way:

> Three years ago, I faced a new season in my life. Overnight I became a widow and single again. The awful sting of death and the heavy circle of loneliness engulfed me every night for months. I dreaded the dark evenings. I remember sitting in my living room in my gold rocking chair, looking at the large brown clock over the fireplace and grieving and sobbing my heart out where no one would hear me. Thank God, I had Roxie, a sweet, rambunctious Australian shepherd puppy, who helped

keep me sane. When asked by friends, "How are you doing?" I would always answer, "I'm taking it one day at a time." I faced questions inside my mind such as, "Is my life working in ministry over, and what good am I now?" Feelings of doubt and unworthiness kept creeping back and trying to overwhelm me. Satan will take every opportunity to place doubt into your life.

In 2016, Kim Haney asked me if I would head a new widows' group. I had just asked the Lord privately that if He wanted me to get involved with the widows of our church to have Sister Haney ask me. Of course, Satan reminded me that I was now in my seventies and that I was getting too old and should slow down. That day she approached me about getting involved with the widows, I knew this was a confirmation. God opened the door to pour my pain into giving to others, and my home has been blessed with these sweet ladies. With our large church, there are over fifty widows, and we meet once a month for lunch and fellowship in my home. This provided an opportunity to meet and get to know these precious women on a very personal basis, because we now have a very special bond, widowhood. Many times we pray together for special needs and always finish around the piano, singing old hymns with the presence of the Lord touching each one. My home is blessed again because I allowed God to use me in my new season.

Fellowship is one of the most needed areas after the loss of a spouse because until this time you have always done everything as a couple. That title has been stripped. It is hard to truly relate unless you have been there. That first Christmas after Jim's death, I was shocked by how many families were at the cemetery. I watched one lady as I was entering the park, standing by a grave crying, and on the way out, she was still there engulfed in grief. This new season, widowhood, did not come with any instructions. I never believed I would be working with widows; this was the furthest thing from my mind. However, God had other plans, and I have always made myself available to Him.

Whatever season of life you are in, give Him your complete commitment. God is not prejudiced. Regardless of whether you are single, married, divorced, or widowed, He can and will use you. All He asks is for a total commitment that will weather the storms of life that come your way. He will open doors no matter what happens in life or what seasons are thrown your way because He knows you are enough.

It doesn't matter what family you came from, if your parents were married, what abuse you have encountered, or what rejection you have faced—your pain was never meant to exceed your purpose, and sometimes you must understand that your purpose will change. You have to allow space for that purpose to change with the changing of seasons. Nothing is allowed to come into your life that does not have some bearing on God's purpose for your life. Some of the hurts, pains, and trials you go through may become the most powerful tools and instruments God will use in your life to minister to others.

Maybe you are reading this right now and you're wondering why that hurtful situation took place in your life—something you did not deserve. Maybe you have questioned secretly why you have been hurt the way you have, why you went through the rejection and pain, why you battle with depression, and why you have the family you do. Let me tell you, God looked at what your purpose was supposed to be for your generation, and He knew you would have the proper tools in your toolbox to be able to be relevant and transparent to those who are hurt and bleeding.

Things in my life have brought much grief and pain, and I have had my own share of battles fighting with bitterness and resentment, but do you know what part of me God uses the most when I'm able to minister to someone? They are the nuggets of gold that God has planted into my soul when I was broken and hurting. They are the broken places inside of me that God has healed and insecurities I have battled with, but here is the secret: God uses those things the most because I have allowed Him to use them. Being transparent is one of the most effective tools God places in our hands to touch others.

You are enough for God to use! No matter what you have faced and gone through in life, God will use everything you have been through for His glory. I don't know what your background is like, I don't know where you come from, but I do know this: God will use everything you have been through. If you aren't willing to step out and trust Him and His plans for your life, you will live your life in vain. If your pain never gets healed, or is never revisited and taken to Jesus, it will exceed your purpose, and you will live out all of life's negative experiences in vain. Your pain was never meant to exceed your purpose, and every time you are able to use what you have been through to help and minister to others, you have lived out the purpose of the pain.

Consider all the heartache Joseph had to go through, living years of painful experiences that he did not deserve. Instead of allowing the hurt and disappointment to take control of his future, he looked at it all through the eyes of faith:

> But as for you, ye thought evil against me; but God meant it unto good, to bring to pass, as it is this day, to save much people alive. (Genesis 50:20)

Joseph knew that God was going to use everything he went through. He looked beyond the curtain of the natural. Even though he could not see specifically how God was going to use all this, he knew God had placed a call upon his life, and whatever was allowed to happen to him was all a part of the plan of God.

Look at what the Scripture says about David after all the mistakes and bad choices he made in his life:

> For after David had done the will of God in his own generation, he died and was buried with his ancestors, and his body decayed. (Acts 13:36, NLT)

Out of everything the Bible could have said about David, all it stated was that he "had done the will of God in his own generation." That's it. It could have said he slayed the giant Goliath and won victory for Israel, he slew the Philistines, he judged Israel, the list could go on. The one heroic and important thing

David accomplished that went down in the hallmark of history was the fact he did the will of God in his generation. He succeeded in the most important accomplishment that outweighed all the others.

You are not an accident, and it was not by chance you were born the year you were born. When all is said and done, all that matters on this earth is that you and I have done the will of God in the time He has allowed us to be used as a vessel for His kingdom! We have to give Him our all. Sometimes it's easy to get caught up in the busyness of life and to look around at the masses of people and secretly think, "Does God really know that I am alive on planet Earth right now? Does God see me?" I want to remind you that just as He saw Jeremiah, He also sees you.

> For I know the thoughts that I think toward you, saith the LORD, thoughts of peace, and not of evil, to give you an expected end. Then shall ye call upon me, and ye shall go and pray unto me, and I will hearken unto you. And ye shall seek me, and find me, when ye shall search for me with all your heart. (Jeremiah 29:11–13)

You have an expected time here on earth. You have an expected purpose. Every day, you will be making choices that will direct your steps on the pathway God has paved for you, or you will make choices that will take you down a different path of life. Every single day. You were set here by God with your personality, your gifts, your strengths, and even your weaknesses so you can serve your generation. My friend, go forth in faith, knowing that God's hand is upon you. With that being enough, you can do anything He places in your heart to do because you are enough.

THE CALL IS TO THE WILLING

In the Hebrews "Hall of Faith" sits a list of imperfect people whom God used. We read all about their heroic deeds, their great faith, and their boldness to come against the enemy, and we in some sense tend to super-humanize these people just because they lived hundreds of years before you and me. We forget about the fact that Noah got drunk, Abraham lied and deceived Abimelech, Sarah laughed and doubted God, Jacob swindled and cheated Esau, Moses murdered an Egyptian, Rahab was a harlot, and Samson consorted with harlots. Peter denied the Lord Jesus, and Paul got into arguments and disagreements with the other apostles. We forget about these things, and even though they are all true, God still used them! In spite of their failures and weaknesses, they had to make the choice within themselves to overcome their failures. When their choice combined with God's call, they did great things for the Kingdom. God still used these imperfect people to obtain promises, stop the mouths of lions, quench the fire of the enemy, and escape the edge of the sword.

If you are going to be effective in your calling, you have to see yourself as God sees you.

God didn't see Adam as just one man alone, but He
saw a world.
Abraham was childless, but God saw a nation.
Jacob was a liar and deceiver, but God saw a Messiah.
Moses was a murderer, but God saw a deliverer.
Gideon doubted and hid from God, but God saw
a great conqueror.
David was just a simple shepherd, but God saw a king.
Peter had no wisdom or filter, but God saw a rock.

When God looks at you, He sees a daughter of God
who will be sold out and in love with Him. As long as
we know who we are and the authority that is given
to us through Jesus Christ, we can be used by God.
You are enough for the call!

4 | *The Call Requires All*

The evidence of a true calling is if you're willing to give it all—everything. God can use only the vessels who are willing to give Him everything: your dreams, your desires, your time, your goals, your image, your self-worth, and your security.

Let's begin with the subject of giving Him your security. I come from a family who has been successful in the business world. My father came from a poor family in the farming district of West Texas, and with determination and hard work he became a successful businessman. While I was growing up, I had that underlying pressure of becoming someone who would follow in his steps and also become successful in finance and business, someone whom my father would be proud of. When the Lord began to call me to a place of ministry, I had to lay the security of pleasing my father on the altar of sacrifice. I don't care how old you are, there is an unseen driving sense of personal security that comes from knowing you have pleased a parent, spouse, or someone who has had a big influence in your life.

Many times I had to revisit that altar when I started to get into various business opportunities that could have been lucrative (even ones that would still allow me to carry the title of ministry), and the temptation of fulfilling that void began to pull inside me. It wasn't so much about making money; it was more about the personal security and self-worth I felt about the job, and the fact that such a job would be viewed as being successful. It was about feeling validated by people who mattered to me versus giving God everything He desired. When we see that God has made our lives His dwelling place and we are chosen vessels of the almighty God, a deep reverence accompanies this calling. When you realize the honor that is bestowed upon you, all frivolity and self-pleasing attributes have to end.

> Know ye not that your body is the temple of the Holy Ghost which is in you, which ye have of God? and *ye are not your own;* for ye are bought with a price: therefore glorify God in your body, and in your spirit, which are God's. (I Corinthians 6:19–20, emphasis mine)

"Ye are not your own." Consecration—total consecration and the death of your own desires—will follow a true call of God. Some will recognize the submission of divine ownership in their lives, but others will remain their own rulers. Not until every area of our lives is totally surrendered to the call of God will He truly operate effectively through us. So you must revisit this question from time to time, "Is every department and every detail of my life living for the Lord's purpose or is any part of me being lived for myself?"

The call of God will require a crucifixion of your desires over and over again; it's not just a one-time go-around. Young lady, middle-aged woman, elder, wherever you are in your season of life, this generation must have women who are willing to sell out to their calling! I do not mean placing your call above your first responsibilities on God's list of priorities (and we will address this subject), but I'm talking about a life that is consumed from the inside out and allows the Lord to fill every inner sanctuary and personal goal. I have sadly watched young women, who evidently had a call of God upon their lives, never be willing to come to the place of laying their personal insecurity and pressure of pleasing others upon the altar of the calling. It meant more to them to have the acceptance of someone on this earth in place of the acceptance that came from knowing they had pleased the One who gave His life for them. A great ministry was aborted due to their choice of pleasing people over pleasing God.

People-pleasing pressures can make us step out of the will of God. Pleasing our own motives and image can make us step out of the will of God. The pressures of our culture can make us miss the will of God for our lives. *Just because everyone else is doing it* can make us miss the will of God!

In Watchman Nee's book, *The Normal Christian Life,* he related a story that touches my heart every time I read it. I would like to share it with you:

> An American friend, now with the Lord, whose name we will call Paul, cherished the hope from his early youth that one day he would be called, "Dr. Paul." When he was quite a little chap he began to dream of the day when he would enter the university, and he imagined himself first studying for his M.A. degree and then for his Ph.D.
>
> The Lord saved him and called him to preach, and before long he became pastor of a large congregation. By that time he had his degree and was studying for his doctorate, but despite splendid progress in his studies and a good measure of success as a pastor, he was a very dissatisfied man.
>
> In his distress he cried to the Lord to cause him to know the power of the indwelling Spirit, but though he had prayed and prayed for months, no answer came. Then he fasted and asked the Lord to show him any hindrances there might be in his life. That answer was not long in coming, and it was this: "I long that you should know the power of My Spirit, but your heart is set on something that I do not wish you to have. You have yielded to me all but one thing, and that one thing you are holding yourself—your Ph.D."
>
> To you or me it might be of little consequence whether we were addressed as plain "Mr. Paul" or as "Dr. Paul," but to him it was his very life. . . . So he reasoned with the Lord in this wise: "Is there any harm for me to be a doctor of philosophy? Will it not bring much more glory to Thy Name to have a Dr. Paul preaching the gospel than a plain Mr. Paul?"

But God does not change His mind, and with all Mr. Paul's reasoning it did not alter the Lord's word to him. Every time he prayed about the matter he got the same answer. All the while Mr. Paul was becoming more and more hungry to know the fullness of the Spirit. This state of affairs continued to within two days of his final examination. God made it clear that he must choose between the power he could sway through a doctor's degree and the power of God's Spirit swaying his life. That evening he yielded. "Lord," he said, "I am willing to be plain Mr. Paul all my days, but I want to know the power of the Holy Ghost in my life."

He rose from his knees and wrote a letter to his examiners asking to be excused from the examination on Monday, giving his reason. The next morning he told his congregation that for the first time in six years he had no sermon to preach and explained how it came about. The Lord blessed that testimony more abundantly than all his well-prepared sermons, and from that time God owned him in an altogether new way. From that day he knew separation from the world, no longer merely as an outward thing but as a deep inward reality, and as a result, the blessedness of the Spirit's presence and power became his daily experience.[4]

It may not be a doctorate degree that is your controversy with God; it may be something totally different. It's a strange thing how God sometimes allows our complete surrender to His call to become dependent upon that *one thing*. God will wait for that one thing. It will haunt us inside our spirit day after day, because He must have our all. But when we truly surrender our lives, great anointing and power can flow! That life will become a vessel capable of great use and influence in the Kingdom. Watchman Nee went on to say, "Not until we take the place of a servant can He take His place as Lord. He is not calling us to devote ourselves to His cause; He is asking us to yield ourselves unconditionally to His will. Are you prepared for that?"

Claudette Walker makes this statement regarding her calling as a young girl:

> My dad was president of the Tupelo Children's Mansion from the time I was four years of age until I was nineteen. My growing-up years were spent around hurting children who were either orphans or had parents who could not or would not raise them. Out of my unique environment, I was given a gift of compassion. I can recall sitting on the mansion's property and listening to the children's stories, which would make me cry. A deep desire to truly help them was born in my spirit. I cared for them deeply but simply had no tools to help them other than a loving arm around their shoulders, genuine tears of compassion, and words of assurance that God loved them. I was fifteen years old when I heard the voice of the Lord late one night in our home on the mansion's grounds. I clearly heard the voice of the Lord say to me, "I am calling you to teach My Word." I did not know this at the time, but my passion to help the hurting mansion kids had been answered with a call to teach His Word.
>
> This meant a major change of plans for my life. My lifelong love for words had caused me to create a plan for my life, which involved getting a PhD and becoming a professor of English literature at an Ivy

League college. However, through a life-threatening illness, God rerouted my training to Apostolic Bible Institute, where I fell in love not with English literature but with the life-changing Word of God. My original plan was to attend Bible college for one year until my health improved, but I ended up graduating from Apostolic Bible Institute.

For some, maybe higher education is God's will, but He never called me to pursue it. However, in ways I would never have chosen, the Lord gave me His own version of a PhD. Through much physical and emotional suffering, the Lord has brought me to secret places where I *privately have dominion* and then He will send me on missions of His choosing where I *publicly have deliverance* for people, which only comes from the hand of the Lord. When I said "yes" to His call at age fifteen, I would probably not have answered "yes" if I had known the price would be so steep. He told me that a call would cost us all! A true calling from the Lord to minister His Word publicly to His people will cost you everything . . . but, oh, the reward to see lives affected for eternity through His powerful Word is worth every step of sacrifice.

Jesus Himself worked as a carpenter during His growing-up years, but once He reached the place where the Spirit called Him into full-time ministry, we do not ever read that He picked up the carpenter's tools again.

Simon Peter and Andrew his brother "left their nets" when Jesus called them to follow Him (Matthew 4:20).

James and John were in the boat with their father, mending their fishing nets, when Jesus called them to

follow Him. The Scriptures tell us, "And they immediately left the ship and their father, and followed
him" (Matthew 4:22).

Many of you reading this book will be mightily
used by God, but here is the basis for it all: God will
use you based on your sold-out choices. God uses
someone by the choices and level of dedication she is
willing to give. He will not use someone He cannot
trust. He will not reach for the vessel that is always
questioning holiness or walking the fence line when
it comes to loving truth and doctrine. God's choice
for you is based solely on your willingness to give
Him all, and He will test you in this area to see how
much He can trust you with first because *He must own
you*. Pray over your mind, and ask the Lord to help
you make the right choices so you can be mightily
used by Him. Let something be birthed inside you
that makes you willing to be totally consumed with
the call of God upon your life.

Even David knew the importance of giving God
a sacrifice that had a price tag attached. After David
had sinned and numbered the people out of disobe-
dience, the Lord spoke to the prophet Gad, who was
David's personal seer, and told David to build an altar
in the threshing floor of Araunah the Jebusite.

David did not own any of this man's land and had
planned to purchase the threshing floor from Araunah
so he could build this altar and offer the sacrifices God
required, in the place God had specified. This was in
order to stop the plagues that were killing the people
of the land. Araunah, being a good man, offered to

give this piece of land to David the king, along with any amount of oxen needed for the sacrifices. This was David's reply:

> And the king said unto Araunah, Nay; but I will surely buy it of thee at a price: neither will I offer burnt offerings unto the LORD my God of that which doth cost me nothing. So David bought the threshingfloor and the oxen for fifty shekels of silver. (II Samuel 24:24)

First Chronicles 21 also relays this story and notes that David bought the threshing floor for "six hundred shekels of gold by weight" (verse 25). David knew enough about the Lord's character to realize it would be dishonorable to God to offer a sacrifice without cost.

If a piece of land was that important, how much more should those who have been called with the highest calling known to humankind be prepared to pour their lives into the call? I am not talking to those who want be used in some area of the church or a ministry extension, but I am addressing those who feel God is calling them to ministry. The call will necessitate a higher level of commitment and release of personal dreams and goals. The ministry will entail a total surrender. But the rewards are unending and worth every mile.

The story of Elijah passing his mantle to Elisha in I Kings 19 sends a powerful signal to those who feel the call of God upon their lives. God spoke to Elijah at the entrance of the cave that day and told him of a specific young man by the name of Elisha, his place of residence, and his parents' identity. I'm sure Elisha had known there was a touch of God upon his life, but when the time came for him to move forward in his ministry, he never tried to keep his former occupation.

> So he departed thence, and found Elisha the son of Shaphat, who was plowing with twelve yoke of oxen before him, and he with the twelfth: and Elijah passed by him, and cast his mantle upon him. And he left the oxen, and ran after Elijah, and said, Let me, I pray thee, kiss my father and my mother, and then I will follow thee. And he said unto him, Go back again: for what have I done to thee? And he returned back from him, and took a yoke of oxen, and slew them, and boiled their flesh with the instruments of the oxen, and gave unto the people, and they did eat. Then he arose, and went after Elijah, and ministered unto him. (I Kings 19:19–21)

The fact that Elisha turned around and slaughtered those yoke of oxen symbolizes the fact when God calls you to a certain place of ministry you cannot hold hands with your dream occupation, vocation, or career. I may have stepped on some toes with that statement because a secular mentality is attacking the church of God with the lie that the call to ministry is a by-product of our vocational pursuits. We want to follow the call of God, but we don't want to sacrifice for it or allow anything to change in our lives.

Think of it this way: if you were studying to become a brain surgeon, there is no way you would ever obtain a reputable degree or reputation as a certified brain surgeon if, at the same time, you continued your studies in law. Wanting to be a successful brain surgeon and also wanting to be a successful lawyer would eventually produce one big failure at either end. These two vocations both require total commitment and single-vision dedication, so how much more does a calling of the highest degree require? Too many people categorize the call to ministry as a second-degree calling and continue with their dreams and careers as if the call of God was of lesser importance when actually it is the highest of all possibilities known to humankind. When God calls a vessel for His glory, it's all or nothing!

Jesus plainly stated:

> No man, having put his hand to the plough, and looking back, is fit for the kingdom of God. (Luke 9:62)

I believe this verse refers to the plow Elisha once held in his hand before Elijah threw his mantle upon him (which symbolized the call of God). Those who are heeding the call to ministry must come with a heart that is willing to give all into the hands of God, for the call of God upon a woman's life is everything or nothing. The one who agrees to answer the call of the ministry but is not willing to let go of the desires and plans she made before the call is not fit for the kingdom of God. You cannot serve your own interests and at the same time serve the interests of God.

Claudette Walker makes this statement regarding the importance of giving all:

> The first sacrifice required is our own plans, desires, and dreams. One of my favorite sayings is this: "God's dreams for your life will put your best dreams to shame!" My personal dream of being "Dr. Kloepper" and teaching English in an Ivy League college was replaced with God's dream for me in speaking His Word to precious people all over the world. When I was young and struggling with giving up my own agenda, the Lord gave me a dream. In the dream I was determined to go one direction. I was tightly clutching something in my hand that, to me, was very valuable, a great treasure I was holding. I heard the Lord calling me from behind, but I knew that in order to follow Him I had to let loose of my treasure. It was so hard, but I finally opened my hand. To my great surprise, I had been clutching a handful of sand. I laughed as I watched the sand seep through my fingers to the ground.
>
> Oh, the true treasures that the Lord has put in my hand since then! I have had the joy of seeing lives changed for eternity. I have watched in amazement as His powerful Word spoken by my feeble voice has been received by hearts and with His Spirit has transformed them. I have precious friends all over the world who have joined with us in spirit and in ministry. You simply are not able to dream big enough for your life!
>
> The second sacrifice you will make is your time. Your time becomes His time. The Lord will be your calendar master. Doing it on your own will lead to utter exhaustion and weariness of spirit because there are always endless needs and people

you should help. I have found that Jesus is not a cruel taskmaster, for His yoke is truly easy and His burden is light. If we are yoked with Him, He will pull the heavier part of the load. We will simply go and serve at His direction. There have been many times I have missed His signal and have gone off on my own agenda, and I can tell you that it never ended well. When I pray first and then obey, He sets the pace and uses (but never abuses) me.

The third sacrifice is money. Many of us could be involved in secular careers and be sitting on easy street financially. Often in ministry we must sacrifice the financial future we could secure on our own and trust God with our finances; this is often the hardest sacrifice to make. When we faithfully tithe and joyfully give money to the kingdom's causes, I have watched the Lord surprise us with houses and cars and vacations that were from *His hand*. Sacrificing our agenda, our time, and our money for ministry has brought such added blessing that even to call them sacrifices seems a stretch. The Lord does require our total allegiance in every area. He told me once, "Claudette, your call will cost you all!"

There may be times during the waiting and preparing process when you must work to pay the bills; there are times a home missions pastor must secure a job in order to pay the rent. We are addressing someone who wants to be successful in both a worldly career and full-time ministry. You cannot be successful in both because one of them will suffer, and the kingdom of God will be the one neglected. I keep hammering at this because a secular mentality has affected the thinking of the church. Wouldn't Satan love nothing more than for God's chosen vessels to be diverted from the intent of His calling and pulled in various areas to the place they are no longer effective? That is exactly his plan!

But think what God can do with a vessel that is totally sold out to Him:

> But as it is written, Eye hath not seen, nor ear heard, neither have entered into the heart of man, the things which God hath prepared for them that love him. (I Corinthians 2:9)

God will use you in ways you cannot even dream about. The sacrifice of giving Him your all will burn in His nostrils day and night as a sweet-smelling savor because there is nothing as powerful as a living sacrifice.

One of the most touching accounts of someone willing to give all to the call of ministry was spoken by one of my dear friends, Sister Bobbye Wendell. I pray this gets hold of your heart like it does mine, and that you allow God to talk to you through her story:

> My husband and I, along with our four children, were appointed missionaries to Ethiopia in 1966. Our deputation would become a two-year ordeal of awaiting visas for entrance into Ethiopia. During the two years of waiting, we again faced a great trial. My husband, Brother Wendell, was in an auto accident, and I was told he would probably not recover. If he did recover he would never walk again without help. I found a place of prayer at the hospital, and as I poured out our need again, God was faithful to answer. A great visitation of

God's help and presence surrounded us, and our call was confirmed again by my husband walking out of that hospital, aided by crutches but only for a while. We were back on our way to Ethiopia.

In November 1968, my husband left for Ethiopia. His visa came in before the children's and mine. It was hard to see him go, but there was so much to do before the children and I would leave in January. We shared our last Christmas in the United States with friends and family and prepared our things for departure. My parents were so broken, for they expected us to be gone from four to six years. That is a long time to be away from your grandchildren.

During the weeks my husband was in Ethiopia, he stayed at the YMCA, and during his stay he met many students of a technical college who frequented the YMCA for several programs they offered. Those students took part in numerous projects that were approved by the school to help the poor and needy of Ethiopia. One of these projects involved an area where victims of Hansen's disease (leprosy) lived. Leprosy causes the nerves to die. Body extremities, such as hands, feet, and nose, would simply disappear or wither away.

It would be impossible to describe the living conditions of those "untouchables." The lepers crowded together in submission to their rejection to society. They were born, lived, married, gave birth, and died just as everybody does. They created their own culture and society and accepted one another. Some slept in holes dug into the ground, some in shacks made of cardboard and pieces of tin and wood. They were rejected by society, but God had a plan that would be revealed to give at least some of these people a glimpse of His love. My husband had been invited to be a part of the group who would attempt to improve the living quarters of these tragic people.

The long flight took us to New York, Rome, and on to Ethiopia. I cannot describe to you the feeling of landing in a strange land, among a strange people and language, yet feeling as if I had come home. The children and I landed in Ethiopia, where we reunited with my husband. It was good to have the family back together. The next day my husband wanted to show me the project he had been working on. We left the children to rest and drove to the area. I was left in the vehicle while my husband went over an embankment and out of sight.

All of a sudden, people began to gather, pushing close to the open window. They had white, gauzy shawls (part of the national dress) around them and across their faces. I noticed they had deformed hands or no fingers and sometimes no hands, only stubs at the end of their arms. I was frozen with absolute fear when the shawls were lowered. Some of them had disfigured faces, no eyebrows, and their noses almost gone. I had never seen anything like it in my entire life. There was nothing that could have prepared me for this. I prayed for my husband to return, and when he did walk back he was surrounded by several of the men. He was laughing and saying strange words that I could not understand, and I wondered how he could be so happy in this type of surrounding. I found out much later.

My husband got into the car and tried to tell me what he was doing, but I told him I just wanted to go home. He stopped laughing, looked at me, and said, "We are home, Bobbye. We have prayed for nine years to get here. We are home and these people are the ones God has given us to start with. If there will be a church in Ethiopia, it will start here." I feebly told him I just wanted to go where the children were, back to the house. I was up all night that night visiting the rooms of my children and asking God and myself, "What have I done?"

The next day, my husband insisted we all go back to the project. The children were still adjusting to the culture; they were about to find out what culture shock really meant. We put huge plastic buckets on top of our Land Rover jeep, and when they were tied down, we all loaded in and drove away. The buckets were for collecting food scraps from the back door of the Hilton hotel. My husband had arranged for the gift of this food that hotel residents left on their plates after finishing. This would be used to feed very hungry people.

We arrived at the assigned place, and planks were laid over sawhorses to make tables. The buckets were placed on the tables as the people began to line up. Their food containers were tin cans, dirty rags, and plastic bags or whatever they could find. They pushed against each other to be first in line to ensure there would be something for them to eat. The noise was terrible; there was shouting, pushing, children crying, and everyone making noise of some kind.

My two daughters were to dip out the food with large spoons. They looked so beautiful that day, with their long hair around their faces and tears washing down their cheeks from fear and pity. Not one word was spoken among us all the way back home. Even our youngest, who was only nine years of age, said nothing. Our oldest sat sheltering his little brother. When we arrived at the house

I started talking, trying to make the atmosphere lighter. I said I would make a special dinner that night. They each said, "I do not want anything to eat; I just want to see my Mamaw and Papaw." That night there was no evening meal, but there were many tears.

Closed off from the bedrooms to prevent disturbing our children, I cried and prayed through the night. Several times I visited their beds, very gently laying my hands upon each one and praying, "None of these diseases, O Lord! None of these diseases!" We were only allowed to preach in certain areas, as dictated by the government. To fulfill this requirement, we rented an old building on a large compound. We dug a hole in the front yard, extracted the dirt, and mixed it with straw purchased off the backs of donkeys as they trotted past the gate with their drivers. This building would house our leper workshop and training center. We hired teachers who would teach cloth weaving, basket weaving, and rug weaving during the day. The site of our church services and evangelical outreach would be our first such building other than our home.

Those victims of leprosy, who were beggars on the streets during the day, began to line up at the gate of the workshop chapel, asking for entrance into the program. Some of them were simply ravaged by the disease; others were not so horribly scarred. I do not know how they found out the workshop was open, but they came, sometimes lining up down the hill to the river waiting for an opportunity to come in. There were five hundred thousand people with leprosy in Ethiopia. There was no end.

After ten months and no one yet baptized, I was desperate for God to do something in this diamond field of humanity. We had 7:30 AM chapel services five days a week, many days of training, preparation of a hot meal of lentils and native bread for the students and workers, and even the task of washing the feet of those who had ulcers so severely on their feet. My husband had huge pans for this. He would wash the feet of the men and put salve on them and bind them. The binding would be saturated the next day to be done over again. We learned what ministry means.

We secured a teacher from within the lepers with whom we could teach the children of the leper families. Evening was welcomed each day as the longing for harvest in this land became unbearably heavy. I knew something had to happen. On the mission field, it is essential to have help in your home. Some household duties there require much extra labor, and I needed help in my home. When my husband drove in one day with the smiling lady looking toward me from the back seat of the vehicle, I knew help had arrived. She smiled all the way in, where I was introduced to her. I had her start in the kitchen, and as she turned to enter the kitchen, I saw the huge ulcer on her leg. My heart sank. I looked at my husband as I walked to the back room and asked, "Does she have leprosy?" He looked squarely at me and said, "Yes." I was horrified! "You brought her into this house with our children? This cannot be!" I told him. "You have to take her away." He said she had no place to go and would be hurt again. She had been beaten terribly by other beggars. Still I looked at him and emphatically said that she had to go. He turned toward me and sadly said, "You may take her, and here are the keys. But will you do something for me?" I asked what it was that he wanted. He asked me if I would go by Calvary on the way to taking her back.

I was numb. Didn't he know that I had been to Calvary? I had been there before but it had been to take a soul to Calvary, not to lead one away. I started to cry. I took the keys from his hand and grabbed my prayer shawl. I flew out of the house but did not take that lady with me, for it was time for something to happen for me that day. Today would be the day.

To drive to the workshop and chapel was not far; it consisted of a road winding down the mountainside and through the village market. The narrow road was crowded with people who seemed to have nothing to do. Every time we drove down without incident was either a tribute to our driving skills or a complete miracle. This day was no exception as I arrived safely at the workshop. It was Saturday. Only the guard was there. His name was Wolde Gabriel, and Wolde had very little of his nose left on his face. I knew he wondered what I was doing there that day. I drove past him to the front door of the building and exited the car.

When you have over one hundred people with various forms of disease and infection eating at them, hands, feet, faces, and bodies, a clinging odor permeates the area. This smell never went away. Soap, disinfectant, and cleaners just added to the strength and intensity of the smell. A smell of dying flesh followed people who had been told that they had no soul, could never get to Heaven, and were never allowed into the vast compounds of the existing state church. Many of these people would sit outside the compound of the state church, waiting for those who participated to leave and, in so doing, hoping the attendees would bless them.

I went deeper into the building. The guard, Wolde, remained at the door. His hands, or whatever remained of them, were held behind his back covered in ulcers. I never touched them, and today was no different. I took my prayer shawl and spread it on the floor where I would kneel to pray, and when I went home I would throw it in the washer before using it again. I just hoped it would last the length of our term in Ethiopia.

I started to kneel and quite firmly announced to the Lord that I had come to be "broken." With that announcement, I went to my knees and started to pray. I was once again reminded that heavy smells can actually be tasted, and the smell was terrible that day. I prayed and nothing happened. After a while, as I attempted to break through, the Lord spoke to me and said, "If you really wish to have your request (to be broken), then remove the prayer shawl."

The thought of my flesh actually touching that floor was overwhelming. Some of the lepers had walked barefoot daily on that floor, and the smells of their infection engulfed the plank flooring. I could not do it. I decided to ignore the voice and continue to pray until the voice came again, "Move the shawl." Finally, I moved the shawl, but the Lord was not finished with me yet.

As I knelt there wondering if there was anything worthwhile in me, this fearful person, the Lord spoke again. "Get down." I stooped a bit but the voice spoke again, "Go down," and I stooped even lower. Finally, after the third time, I tearfully asked the Lord, "I'm down . . . how much further?" He said, "Until there is no further down." I went down and stretched my body and face to the floor of that chapel as I laid before the

Lord with weeping. At times I would feel to turn my face but then I would understand that I was to stay where I was. Something was happening. About three hours later it was like a dam broke inside me as fear of disease and strangeness poured from inside me. From the lower regions of my body, the flowing out of sounds and words from my mouth, the Lord delivered me there that day. I would never be the same again. There would be a harvest and a church in Ethiopia!

I arose from that place a new person and went outside the building. The guard simply looked at me as I said, "Wolde, give me your hands." He held them behind his back. I asked him again, and finally he extended them toward me. I took his hands in mine, and I said to him, "You will never have to hide your hands from me again." And he never did.

The foundation of the enemy's resistance was broken that day, and soon we would baptize our first Ethiopians in the name of Jesus. In those beginning days of harvest, twenty-seven lepers were baptized in Jesus' name and several received the Holy Ghost.[5]

How can we expect one generation to give their all to the call of God and not expect the same from the next generation? We cannot steal and embezzle the experience of the true power and anointing of God from the previous generation just because we are unwilling to give all! God will use vessels who are wholly surrendered to Him and His calling and willing to go the distance and do what it takes for His power to be made manifest in the earth. My friend,

God will test you to see if you are serious about the call. He will test you to see if you can be trusted with such a great treasure.

In the days of the Old Testament, when the people of God were in desperate need for the power of God to be demonstrated, they would build a stone altar. But the altar itself was not enough; God would not visit a vacant altar until it became the home of a sacrificed lamb or bull. Only when there was a sacrifice involved would God step on the scene and show forth His power in their midst. Only the pain, blood, and death of a sacrifice would cause God to answer the needs of His people.

If you are serious about God using you as a powerful vessel that will be effective in the realm of the Spirit and in the lives of other people, you must be willing to sacrifice your dreams and your plans. A vessel that has surrendered itself to God but refuses to pay a debt of sacrifice will never become effective for His kingdom. The calling itself will not bring an anointing. The calling must be nurtured and fed through a consistent prayer life and seasons of consecration through fasting and drawing closer to God.

Only a vessel that is willing to lay herself (this is not something God will do for you) on the altar of sacrifice will truly see the fire of God fall upon her life and ministry.

Donna Linville addresses the importance of being sold out to the call:

I think the biggest hindrance to a woman who feels the call of ministry upon her life is the misplacement of self. If *self* is dominating your spirit, if *self-image or stature* is predominant in your priorities and your need to become something or prove yourself to someone else, you will become your greatest hindrance to God being able to use you. God does not glory in human flesh.

I have to be honest and say that early in my ministry I probably would have enjoyed the height of my ministry, but God in His wisdom disintegrated that as quickly as it happened. Instantly. The place you have to keep coming back to is the question, "Who is on the throne?" I constantly had to make sure He was first and foremost in every area of my life. God also made sure of this through circumstances He would allow in my life. Every time I would come to a crossroad or something would start pulling me another direction, I would hear Him say, "Lovest thou Me more than all of these?" The "these" He was referring to included what others thought of me, the pleasure in being uplifted, and the desire to be recognized—the sacrifice of the calling.

The sacrifice of the calling demanded I give up certain things that I wanted to keep. Even though I felt God wanted me to sacrifice certain things on the altar, I wanted to maintain and keep possession of certain things that I knew God was asking of me, but I still wanted have the God-given anointing and effective ministry. I am sixty-five at the time of this writing, and I have to constantly reestablish that altar of "Lovest thou Me more than all of these?" The reason is because He makes us who we are supposed to be only when He is allowed to be Lord of all in our lives. I cannot say that in my life it has always been that way, but God has constantly reminded me that He is on the throne when my flesh or desires start to arise. They have to be laid down again as a sacrificial offering to the Lord. It's something that will take place at every level and every season of your life.

One of the greatest sacrifices I had to lay on the altar was acceptance of the fact that I was not able to have children. I was pursuing adoption, and whether God wanted me to have a child or not didn't matter. I was *going* to adopt a child.

My prayer life at that time became somewhat diminished because I would go to prayer, and then God would take me in the Spirit to the room of surrender. To be completely honest with you, I didn't want to go to the room where I had to surrender to His will in this area, so I would mute that prayer. In my times of prayer, I would avoid that room of surrender and keep my focus from going there. Then, God would withdraw His Spirit from me because He wanted me to surrender to His will so He could use me. Looking back now, God knew what my particular path in life would hold. Only God understood that for His will to be completely accomplished and for the ministry He had in store for me and my own good, I could not be diversified. He knew I could not handle all of the other responsibilities and expenditures for my lot in life. If I had a child I would have focused solely on that.

It always goes back to that little nine-year-old girl standing at the altar, surrendering my life to God to be whatever it is He wants me to be. Not being able to have a child was probably one of my biggest sacrifices in regard to doing the will of God. I have gone through cancer and surgeries. I even adopted a child one time and ended up losing it back to the system. But with every turn of the road, in the midst of pain and hurt was the voice, "Lovest thou Me more than all these?" I have gone through seventeen surgeries and the disappointment of adopting and losing a child. I tried to get a child from Tupelo Children's Mansion, and that opportunity fell through. Every level of disappointment required the original call of: "Lovest thou me more than these?" These things were required for *me*. Not everyone goes through the same level of sacrifice, but *it will be something* if God has truly called you.

For me, holiness has never been an issue. I have never been tempted to hold that back from God, but what I had envisioned my future embracing and becoming included children and I could never have it. For some divine reason, it was not meant for me to have those things, so I had to release them to the One I loved then and still love "more than all of these." If God's hand is upon your life and you have been called, you will not have the opportunity from God to mold your own future.

I don't think anyone could say it any better. It's not just a one-time sacrifice when you're laying over an altar somewhere after a convicting message and you say "yes" to God and "yes" to His calling, but your calling and your level of commitment will be tested again and again. Sometimes it's not such a major sacrifice as giving up the possibility of having a child, but it may come in the small things, which sometimes carry just as much weight because they seem so insignificant.

We don't know what is truly inside our own hearts; that is why we have to trust the One who does. Jesus will make a visit to the house of your heart at awkward times and unexpected moments just to see if your commitment to the call is still strong and secure. He will ask things of you that may not mean anything to someone else but could stand in the way of your calling. The Lord tested Hezekiah, literally at a time in his life when he was most prosperous. Hezekiah had been instrumental in turning God's people back to worshiping the one true God when idols filled the land. The Bible says, "He left him," as in God actually stepping aside, standing back, and watching Hezekiah from a distance to see how he would respond.

> Howbeit in the business of the ambassadors of the princes of Babylon, who sent unto him to enquire of the wonder that was done in the land, God left him, to try him, that he might know all that was in his heart. (II Chronicles 32:31)

God will do that in the lives of those He trusts to carry His gospel. You are a special vessel that must remain poured out and emptied so the anointing can flow through you. Hindrances at all levels will be tested, and God's spotlight will shine brightly upon them so they can be exposed in our lives. The Lord will test us, just as He did Hezekiah, to see what is really going on inside our hearts. There have been times in my life when the Lord has tested me to see what was in my heart.

Many of these things were personal "convictions," I guess you could say, but for me they were levels of commitment to the call. Several years ago, we were in the middle of a building program, and my father-in-law was the pastor at that time. He had brought in an evangelist to help raise money and ask people to commit to pledges. Conviction was hot that night. He preached about giving sacrificially for the kingdom of God, and people were bringing their computers, china sets, televisions, and committing their boats, cars, and all kinds of personal items. In this service the Lord asked me to give my mink coat that had been a special gift to me on my thirtieth birthday from my parents.

Nobody in the world would have ever known if I refused to give it, but God would have known. That was all that mattered. It wasn't so much the coat but the fact it had been a special gift that was sentimental to me. That afternoon I went home, wrapped it in the fabric cape that protected it, drove to the church, and when nobody was around, I laid that coat upon the altar. Now, do you think God (or the church for that matter) really needed that coat? Of course not. A used mink coat does not sell for much on eBay. But something of much more value was proven that day I laid the coat upon the altar. I was letting the Lord know, "Whatever it is You ask of me, whether small or great, I am willing to release it to You." Jesus saw something much greater that day than a mink coat.

Many times, the Lord has asked me to empty out my personal savings account and give the entire amount to missions or some need that was presented. There have been times the Lord has asked us to sell our home and give to missions. Sometimes it will be small things. Other times He will ask larger things of you. Like Paul, if you are going to walk worthy of the call, you have to learn to live victoriously in either extreme:

> I know what it is to be in need, and I know what it is to have plenty. I have learned the secret of being content in any and every situation, whether well fed or hungry, whether living in plenty or in want. (Philippians 4:12, NIV)

YOU REPRESENT THE CALL

The vocational world has a slogan that states: *Dress for the job you want.* It's a powerful statement that conveys a simple truth: It *does* matter what you wear to work. Not only do your clothes affect your confidence, but people make snap judgments about your abilities based on what you're wearing.

One study conducted in 2014 at Yale, for example, revealed that men who wear suits are better at negotiating than those wearing street clothes or sweats. In the study, the more casually-dressed participants backed down more quickly and weren't taken as seriously as their suited-up counterparts. In another study, published last year, men wearing more formal office clothes tended to exhibit stronger leadership skills than those who were dressed casually. The formally dressed participants were better at abstract thinking and focusing on the big picture while the less dressed-up folks tended not to be taken as seriously.

First impressions are powerful. According to psychological studies published in *Business Insider,* a person's first impression of you is formed within seven to seventeen seconds of first meeting you, and those seven to seventeen seconds will account for 55 percent of that person's opinion of you.

In the secular world, living and dressing for the career you want is important because success requires that everything about what you're doing be consistent with your goals and aspirations. So much of the time, the way you're presenting yourself through what you put on your body, is what matters most. If you want to be an entrepreneur, you have to align the way you look with that concept. If you want to be a doctor, the first step is to put your physical appearance in line with that goal. When you dress for the career you want, you embody everything about that particular career. You internalize it. Instead of dreaming about maybe becoming something or someone one day, you literally become what you are destined to become. When you aspire to do something, it's not just a want; it's a belief.

If the secular world understands this powerful fact of how our clothes speak for us, how much more for the woman who is called by God to represent the kingdom of God? This doesn't refer simply to dressing in a conservative way. Your clothing not only represents you, but also your calling. Allow me to share a somewhat embarrassing story of how I learned this lesson the hard way.

As a young minister's wife, I loved high fashion and daring wardrobes (although I always made sure to keep them godly). My mentality was, *the more bling the better,* with the bold colors and unique outfits that lined the shelves and racks of my closet as evidence. In my immature mentality, I was determined that I was not going to become my mother-in-law or any of the other older ladies who always dressed in a style I thought of as the "in-the-box preacher's wife." I was determined I was not going to be put in a box just to please other people. I was going to be myself. I was not going to fit the mold, and I was out to prove it to the world.

I will never forget the Ladies' Landmark service with thousands of women in attendance. I marched across that long platform to the pulpit in a black fringe skirt that swished and swayed every time I walked and a pair of bright red, high-heeled boots that were immediate eye magnets. I cannot fully describe to you the conviction that came over me that day. No one said anything to me, nobody made a comment or even a compliment, but the Holy Ghost said many things. Really loud. I didn't really know why I felt the way I did, but something inside me was saying that I should not have worn that outfit and those bright red boots. Looking back, I know it was the Spirit of God giving me direction because it was not really about the red boots or fringe skirt—it was about respecting the call of God upon my life. That call must be reverenced and clothed appropriately on that vessel. I never forgot that day and the way I felt as I learned a Holy Ghost lesson.

When you are a woman with a calling of God upon your life, you no longer belong to yourself, and that includes what you desire to put on your body. A number of things must be surrendered and laid at the feet of the Master, whom you serve, that others are not asked to give up. The call has many sacrifices, and sometimes the hardest part is staying within a personal conviction when others, who do not have that call, are allowed to do things or dress in a manner that you cannot.

The call of God upon your life is a serious thing, and our dress and outward appearance must match that. I immediately know a nurse by the scrubs and shoes she wears, or a military officer by the beautifully designed and stately suit he is clothed in. You and I are called to the highest office obtainable on this earth, so why should we be any different?

I was in the company of several ministers' wives in the middle of a conference when this next example happened. One of the ministers' wives had a thing for high design and fancy dress, taking it to the extent of being over the top, stepping out in outfits that looked like Chanel threw up. But I knew this person and knew there was a good, solid heart and down-to-earth spirit behind the exterior of a high-fashion designer. There was a dear, older woman who was with us, who had been a powerful minister herself for decades and had never met the other women in the group. One evening as we were talking, she made a comment about what a wonderful person and sweet spirit this high-fashion person had. Then she made this statement that has stuck with me: "She is different than whom she alludes."

Your clothes say it all for you even before you get to prove who you are inside. Before even one word comes out of your mouth, before any expression of kindness, your clothes are speaking to others around you about who you are. They are telling on you. And if you do not have the time or opportunity to change that perspective of yourself, they are stuck with that first impression of who you are. You see, it's not really about the clothes; it's about the office of the calling. It's about the call of God you represent.

The Bible is full of examples of God clothing His ministers in certain and specific ways. Even in the very beginning, after the fall of Adam and Eve, it was important to God that they were clothed in a certain way. It was so important, God even made the garments Himself:

> The LORD God made garments of skin for Adam and his wife and clothed them. (Genesis 3:21, NIV)

> Then bring near to yourself Aaron your brother, and his sons with him, from among the sons of Israel, to ministers as priest to Me—Aaron, Nadab and Abihu, Eleazar and Ithamar, Aaron's sons. You shall make holy garments for Aaron your brother, for glory and for beauty. You shall speak to all the skillful persons whom I have endowed with the spirit of wisdom, that they make Aaron's garments

to consecrate him, that he may minister as priest to me. (Exodus 28:1–3, NASB)

The Matthew Henry commentary has this to say about the importance of clothing for ministers:

> These glorious garments were appointed, (1.) That the priests themselves might be reminded of the dignity of their office, and might behave themselves with due decorum. (2.) That the people might thereby be possessed with a holy reverence of that God whose ministers appeared in such grandeur. (3.) That the priests might be types of Christ, who should offer himself without spot to God, and of all Christians, who have the beauty of holiness put upon them, in which they are consecrated to God. Our adorning, now under the gospel, both that of ministers and Christians, is not to be of gold, and pearl, and costly array, but the garments of salvation, and the robe of righteousness.

The Lord told Ezekiel that the levitical priests were required to wear certain garments to minister in. This verse shows us that holiness is made evident by our choices in clothing:

> When they go out into the outer court, into the outer court to the people, they shall put off their garments in which they have been ministering and lay them in the holy chambers; then they shall put on other garments so that they will not transmit holiness to the people with their garments. (Ezekiel 44:19, NASB)

I will never forget the experience as long as I live. My family and I were on a vacation near Monterey,

California, and my girls and I found an awesome, funky, vintage resale shop. It was located in an old, unique home, and as we stepped through the door, I was amazed at the demonic activity present inside that used clothing store. I could not get out of that place fast enough; it felt as if we had stepped inside an ongoing séance as the atmosphere was filled with all types of demonic forces.

The Holy Ghost inside us prompted us to leave, and as we made our way out of that place, I was again reminded that spirits can be connected to pieces of clothing. Since this experience, I have been inside vintage shops that display costumes and performance outfits worn by various performers in years past, and I have sensed the same demonic activity. I don't really understand it all; all I know is that it's real and my spiritual antenna picks up on what is present in the atmosphere. Clothing can be connected to a spirit. As women of God we must be aware of the clothing we put on our bodies and aware of the fact it exudes spiritual, carnal, and sensual vibes to others around us. We make the choice of what type of vibe we want to send.

During our Women in Leadership course at Christian Life College, I present this thought-provoking question to the young ladies who feel a call to ministry: You constantly, at all ages and all seasons of life, have to make the choice: *do I want to be godly or do I want to be sexy?* The culture tells us we can be both, but that is a lie. This is a question that must be answered in a sincere and honest way that is between you and God and revisited again in every season of life. This does not give us a ticket to look frumpy or plain, or to look like we stepped out of the 1800s, but we should dress in our finest that displays the King we represent.

Remember the call requires all. It's not about what others see, but it's what God knows. You and I as women live in a world that screams on every corner we should look a certain way, be a certain weight, live a certain lifestyle, have a certain collection of clothes in our closets, and always look like a model. My friend, that is not reality. As you get older the weight is harder to get off, the hair starts to turn grey, and the energy levels are not there like they used to be as the security of youth starts to fade. Staying secure in whom you represent will carry you through these seasons of change and help you to embrace and accept the changes.

God will hold your hand through every course of life. You will never look back and regret the fact that you gave Him all, but you can look back and regret the times you have not. In Jesus' name, I encourage you to fall at the cross today all over again and surrender your life and dreams to the call Jesus is placing upon you so you can become a powerful and effective tool in this sin-sick world. The times demand sold-out, consecrated, hungry individuals who follow the old paths that produce powerful, anointed ministers.

5 | *The Sacrifices of the Call*

On October 12, 1972, forty passengers were on a nonstop flight from Uruguay to Chile. Among those forty passengers was a rugby team of twenty excited young men who were on their way to being national champions.

Approximately one hour into their flight, strange noises began to erupt inside the plane's transmitter as it rocked back and forth. Suddenly, it took a dive and began to plunge several hundred feet as the plane began a freefall from over two thousand feet midair. The terrified passengers were shattered; some of them were killed instantly as seconds later both wings were torn off by the jagged mountain peaks. The plane came to a crashing halt in the middle of the snowy, forsaken terrain of the Andes Mountains.

Twenty-six of the forty passengers miraculously survived, only to face a slow death from cold and starvation, while the dead were thrown into a snowy grave on the other side of the plane. Having no substantial food but only a small supply of cheese and chocolate that someone had brought on the airplane, their bodies began to deteriorate in the below-freezing temperatures as they tried to keep their minds from going insane.

Weeks went by with no sign of rescue. Their hunger began to overtake them and one of them, being a medical intern, knew that the human body could not survive without proteins. With no plant or animal life in close range, he knew nothing could live at that high altitude.

With the hunger that tormented them day and night, combined with their driving desire to live, the fourteen remaining survivors made the desperate decision that they would live on the flesh of the dead. Yes, cannibalism.

As the medical student began to filet the flesh of the arms and legs of the dead, they each took small portions, rolled them in the chocolate that was left, and swallowed the pieces whole while trying not to concentrate on what they were swallowing. But because they lived on human flesh, they lived to tell their story.

You're probably thinking, *Sister Haney, that is gross.* Yes, but when you're driven by hunger, you think differently. Hungry people don't care what others think about them; all they know is they are driven by a powerful force that no one else can relate to unless she has experienced that same hunger. I have conveyed to you through this true story what can happen when a natural hunger takes hold of someone, but now I want to talk to you about what happens when a person called of God becomes hungry for the Spirit.

A spiritual hunger got hold of a twenty-nine-year-old man and pulled him away from his prestigious position as a lawyer to follow the call of God.

Charles Finney—just one man—had such an anointing upon him that great conviction would fall upon the most hardened hearts during his messages. The anointing of God was so great upon him that people sought him throughout the night because of the deep anguish and conviction that gripped their souls as they tried to sleep. It is recorded that because of this man's anointing, people would burst out of their houses as he passed by, begging him to pray and to help them find Christ.

At one time Finney entered a cotton mill where several hundred employees were working. And because of this anointing that rested upon him, one by one, workers began to drop to their knees and burst into tears of repentance. The power of God became so great they ordered the factory to be shut down as the spirit of revival swept that city.

You may say, "I want to see revival like that! I want that powerful anointing that releases supernatural demonstrations. I want to see this kind of change in my world and see those things in my generation!" It's funny how we always hear about the glory, we hear about the results of God being powerful and active, but we don't hear how a hungry man acted behind the scenes. No one wants to talk about the hours this man laid before the Lord in deep travail and intercession. Or, after hours of exhausting preaching, it is recorded that he would be so deeply burdened that the agony would drive him to pray throughout the night.

On one account Charles Finney became so hungry he locked himself in a barn and buried himself in a haystack for three days and nights saying, "God, I will not come out of here until You have answered me." This is why he ministered in revivals where sinners and atheists screamed for mercy.

You see, hungry people do strange things. Hungry people do things that others don't understand. Hungry people walk lonely roads and are familiar with broken places and spent lives. Hungry people cannot be satisfied with the newest ministry techniques; they don't follow the paths of the crowds or fit in with the popular trends of the culture. Hungry people are concerned with nothing besides fulfilling that longing that drives them. Hungry people follow the paths that have been tried and proven from those who have walked before them.

I can tell you about another hungry man and his wife. Brother C. P. Kilgore carried such an anointing upon him that he would walk to the pulpit and not say a word, as the power of God radiated from him into those old brush arbors to such a degree that sinners would come running, screaming to the altar with conviction. Entire communities would become converted, as creative miracles and healings took place day after day.

We want these results and we hunger for this, but we don't talk about the fact that this couple's hunger drove them into seasons of prayer and fasting for days.

For thirty straight days, one of them was praying at every moment. When one would get exhausted, the other would pick up the burden and start to pray—as they prayed day and night without ceasing for thirty days.

That's not easy. That is hard work. The real anointing of God has a price tag attached, and there is no discounted version that will bring the same results. You get what you pay for.

My friend, you and I are walking in a modern religious world that will offer us many options—spiritual fast food is on every corner and it's cheap. It will present options that send a false message such as "you don't have to pay full price" or "the previous generations have paid and sacrificed so you don't have to." When men or women begin to satisfy their hunger with spiritual fast food, they breed spiritual babies who are weak, sickly, diseased, and so addicted to spiritual preservatives that they will never know what the real thing tastes like.

Studying the newest strategies of church growth and putting on religious productions filled with smoke and fancy light shows are much easier and more convenient than crawling into a lonely, dark prayer room and seeking the face of God, but you will not get the same results because there is no substitute for old-fashioned prayer and fasting! There is no substitute for the lonely prayer closet that brings the glory and power of God into a person's life.

Jesus Himself tried to pass on this message to His followers the day a desperate father came to Jesus and His disciples, looking for an answer and help for his boy. Somehow this man's son had opened himself up to some evil spirits, and they were trying to destroy him through a spirit of suicide. The father said these devils had been in him from childhood. Those devils had lived in this boy perhaps for twenty-plus years, and they were not about to give up their territory.

> And when they were come to the multitude, there came to him a certain man, kneeling down to him, and saying, Lord, have mercy on my son: for he is lunatick, and sore vexed: for ofttimes he falleth into the fire, and oft into the water. And I brought him to thy disciples, and they could not cure him. (Matthew 17:14–16)

Apparently, this dad had brought his son to the disciples so they could cast out these demons. They tried everything that had worked for them before, but the demons refused to obey. Jesus' followers were confused as to why the evil spirits could not be cast out of the boy. I am glad this happened to the faithful, dedicated disciples of Jesus that day because through this situation, a great spiritual secret was exposed to every generation to come. Jesus looked at them and said:

> O faithless and perverse generation, how long shall I be with you? how long shall I suffer you? bring him hither to me. (Matthew 17:17)

Notice that Jesus did not call them *powerless,* but He called them *faithless.* Without doubt, the power to cast out demons was there because just a little while earlier, in Matthew 10:1, Jesus had called His disciples together and had given them power against unclean spirits.

So what was going on here? Trust me, the disciples wondered this too. These guys had been chosen and elected by Jesus Himself, and they had already healed the sick, cast out devils, and preached to the crowds with great power. You can sense the heat they were feeling that day as they stood completely baffled and probably somewhat discouraged. After the embarrassment wore off and the crowds began to thin out and go toward their homes that evening, the disciples couldn't wait to get Jesus alone to find out why these spirits refused to be subject to them. There must have been a reason.

> Then came the disciples to Jesus apart, and said, Why could not we cast him out? (Matthew 17:19)

Right here Jesus passed on to them a great spiritual insight that has not changed or been replaced by anything more convenient, logical, or affected by the culture.

> And Jesus said unto them, Because of your unbelief: for verily I say unto you, If ye have faith as a grain of mustard seed, ye shall say unto this mountain, Remove hence to yonder place, and it shall remove; and nothing shall be impossible unto you. (Matthew 17:20)

The answer was because of their unbelief. Notice, it wasn't due to their lack of power, but the demon would not budge because of their lack of faith. This tells us there are various degrees of authority in the spirit realm, and certain demonic spirits are stronger

than others. Jesus was trying to relay to His ministers that something takes place deep inside a person's
faith when physical sacrifices are made in that man
or woman's life. He went on to reveal the spiritual
mixture it takes to possess this type of faith over any
spirits of Hell.

> Howbeit this kind goeth not out but by prayer and
> fasting. (Matthew 17:21)

I didn't say that. Your pastor didn't say that. Jesus
said it. The Word of God just lays it out in front of
us, saying, "If you're hungry for this level of power, if
you're searching for the deep things of the Spirit, if you
want to see the power of God demonstrated in great
measure, it's going to come through nothing else but
by prayer and seasons of fasting." Fasting does not produce power, but it produces *faith*. And faith is the voice
the spirit world must yield to. When prayer is mixed
with times of fasting, it squeezes the unbelief out of our
spirits and allows God's faith to fill us. It makes us more
spiritually sensitive to the voice of God; it makes us
more perceptive as a new boldness is birthed inside. It
brings us out of our natural personality and places upon
us a mantle of anointing that embraces a holy boldness
that cannot be generated on our own.

Prayer mixed with fasting crucifies your flesh as
God's Spirit grows stronger and His voice becomes
more clear. Jesus made it clear that "this kind," or this
kind of devil, this particular level of demonic possession, will not be moved by ordinary faith. It must

be a faith that is birthed through prayer mixed with seasons of fasting.

You may work years to hold a ministry degree in your hand, but that degree will not bring the anointing upon your life. That degree is to be used as a tool in your hand, not as a replacement for your hunger or substitute for sacrifice. Life will always have its ways of trying to strip you of your hunger: pressures, demanding schedules, stress, times of hurt and bitterness, days of discouragement and weariness. These things will try to rob you of your prayer life. But no matter how loud your flesh screams, if you will keep your prayer life strong and mix it with seasons of fasting, it will keep the flame burning that fuels your hunger.

Joy Haney talks about the power that sacrifice brings upon your life:

> There was something about the older generation that was fully committed to the cause of Jesus Christ. I pray that same commitment comes from the generation who comes behind us and that nothing will stand in their way. They will love the truth through thick and thin, rain or shine, trials, demons, Hell, and all kinds of demonic attacks. May this be a generation that will rise and say, "We are taking this ship through to victory and not letting go of anything but prevailing in the name of Jesus Christ."
>
> In 1972, when my father-in-law was suddenly killed in a car accident, we came back to Stockton where they pastored and resumed the pastorate of that church. I began to read about the old revivals

that took place in this nation and beyond as God began to open my eyes and light a hunger inside me. I read *The Phenomenon of Pentecost* by Frank Ewart, books by A. D. Urshan about the early revivals in Wales and the "Fulton Street revival" that lasted three years across America in 1857. I read about Scotland and how these hungry people would pray into the wee hours of the night, and that revival began to spread into New Zealand.

As I read these things, something happened inside me. I began to hunger for revival more than anything in the world; I wanted to witness the glory of God! We couldn't just pastor a church and be normal or babysit saints. We had to have moves of God. One Sunday after my husband's father passed away, my husband got up to a very depressed congregation and told them, "I didn't come back to Stockton to babysit you, but I came back to build a church. We are going to put our grief into the work of God, get out of this sadness, and go to work for Jesus Christ." He started prayer and fasting chains, twenty-four-hour shifts. The church woke up after a while, and God came into that place. Even though we had great battles, something about this hunger drove and propelled us. I remember being around people and feeling this great burden in my soul that was driving me with hunger. I would be talking with people and they thought I was just engaging in conversation, but the cry of my soul burned within me day and night. I remember talking to Sophie Haney, my husband's grandmother, as she would tell me she had heard the heavenly choirs and talk about the old days and how the power of God would manifest. My heart cried for that as I wanted it so badly.

When my husband called 5 AM prayer meetings, we would drag our kids out of bed, our hair wasn't combed very nicely, and it looked like we just crawled out of bed, but it didn't matter because we were going to prayer. It began to grow as a spirit of prayer began to get hold of the church and powerful things began to happen.

One morning a man walked in with a cane with a satanic serpent wrapped around it and began chaining the doors, trying to shut the people out who were coming to the prayer meeting. The people of God began to sense there was something demonic about this and began to pray, "In the name of Jesus." That man picked up his cane and knocked one of our ushers in the head as blood went everywhere, but God healed him and protected him. That demon-possessed man went outside, and on the sidewalk in front of the church and with all of us watching, his body levitated and lifted off the sidewalk about six inches. Then he jumped into his pickup, drove to San Francisco, jumped off the Bay Bridge, and committed suicide. The demons inside him drove him into the waters just like the demons drove the pigs into the water in Gadara.

When you begin to pray and fast and seek after the supernatural, you awaken the devils. Satan doesn't care if we just go through life living a safe, traditional Christian walk. He doesn't care if we come to church to have our little parties and talk sessions, pat one another on the back, and never get stirred with a great hunger. But you let someone get into a red-hot prayer meeting, and the devils get worried. They hate it when the church prays! That's why the demons try to keep us from praying because that is our power with God just as stated in Acts 4:31:

And when they had prayed, the place was shaken where they were assembled together; and they were all filled with the Holy Ghost, and they spake the word of God with boldness. (Acts 4:31)

Prayer gives you power and boldness! After that incident, our youth were having an all-night prayer meeting, and revival had started as God was bringing people into the church. I remember praying one night in the altars, and looking up, I saw a blue cloud over the front of the altar. I knew it was the glory cloud, just a taste of something I had been hungering for. It doesn't matter to God where you are; He will bring revival and great moves of the Spirit if you will begin to pray and fast and seek His face for revival.

If there is some way I can whet the appetite of this younger generation, you can have the same thing. When the Spirit was moving so mightily among us, many of us went on long fasts, and during this time I felt moved by God to write the book, *When Ye Fast*. I felt impressed to call Brother T. W. Barnes and talk to him about this subject. From the mouth of this prophet rolled the most beautiful words from God about fasting and prayer. He said, "Sister Haney, you have hit upon something that is lacking in the church. If we want to see what God wants us to see, we have to get back to the old-fashioned prayer and fasting."

Who will pick up the mantle of sacrifice for their generation? The older generation had miracles, the early Pentecostals had miracles, the early church had miracles, and the church of today *must have miracles* and moves of the supernatural! We can have it. If we desire and pray and sacrifice, we can have it. Is this something that is strange to us? I ask God to bring His church into a new dimension of power and faith—knowing that you have the power to do these things we read in the Book of Acts. It's not about who you are or where you come from, but it's about how much you will let God flow through you. I pray we will get this mentality: "God can use me, and I don't have to be somebody, have a name, or belong to the greatest church." God can take a humble nobody and use him or her.

When people humble themselves and pray, God will do it! The greatest days of revival are before us. Where is our power? We should not have so many sick people among us; we should be praying these sicknesses away so that the Lord would receive all the glory. The world has gone mad and it's ripe for revival. Terrorists stand on every corner, and their one mission is to kill. The church should be just as radical as these terrorists to see people delivered and filled with the Holy Ghost. Suicide bombers are so consecrated to their evil cause they are even willing to die to make it happen, yet some of us cannot even stir out of our comfortable beds in the morning to pray for a world that is going to Hell. God needs you, and even though we are all different and unique in our callings, God does expect the same consecration. He expects people in each generation to be living sacrifices and to take up their cross.

The mantle of the Spirit is not just an heirloom, it's not just a conversation piece, but it's the entrance into the spirit world. It will take you to dark places where you will need to bind spirits and cast out demons. It will take you to sick people, and as you pray they will be raised up by the power of Jesus

Christ. It will take you down corridors of despera-
tion; you will deal with all types of spirits. It's not
about you or me, but it's all of us doing the will of
God on this earth together. And if it's not happening,
we need to make it happen through the mantle of
sacrifice. I pass on to this generation weapons that
have worked for me as well as for those who have
gone before me. You cannot replace them. God
wants you to lay your life on the altar and let go of
the things the world is bidding you to take up.

We sing songs with messages like "use me, God;
I surrender my life; I will do whatever it takes to save
the lost; I hunger for revival," but do we really mean
those words we sing? Do we sing them from our
souls, or do we sing them because they have a good
beat, they are emotionally stirring, and we get caught
up in the moment of the excitement? What you do
with those prayers that have been put to music reveals
what is inside your heart.

Do you put forth the effort on a daily basis to
spend time alone with God? Do you set aside times
of consecration, away from the crowds, away from
fun and entertainment, to fast and seek the Lord? Or
are you too busy? Are you a stranger to the lonely
place in God? Is the prayer closet filled with spiritual cobwebs? Singing a song, lifting your hands,
even allowing tears to run down your cheeks are
not enough to make a difference. It's what you do
with those prayers, it's the choices you make, and
it's the crowds you run with and voices you allow
to speak into your life. Let me be the first to tell you

that ministry is a lonely life, and you feel the sting of it over and over again. The solitary path is not a one-time place you visit.

LONELINESS OF THE CALL

You will carry the cross of sacrifice when you carry the call to ministry. You will feel the weight of that cross when others have parties and everyone is invited but you. It's not due to the fact they don't like you or enjoy your company, but it is part of the *sacrifice* of the calling. Others see you as different, not that you're any better than anyone else, but the call will bring a certain separation. A minister must accept that fact and understand the loneliness of the call. The loneliness of the call was no stranger to Jesus as Luke records.

> Yet the news about him spread all the more, so that crowds of people came to hear him and to be healed of their sicknesses. But Jesus *often withdrew to lonely places and prayed.* (Luke 5:15–16, NASB, my emphasis)

The call must be protected and guarded, and there are some places you will not be able to go. There will be people *you* cannot hang out with. You will be engulfed by the calling and take on the identity of the call. When you embrace this call, you are no longer your own. You don't have the right anymore to make your own choices or follow your own desires, and I don't necessarily mean worldly or carnal desires but even personal goals. You become dead to yourself and your own ambitions and die at the foot of the cross to your own agenda. You cannot do what others do. There is a high price of loneliness that accompanies the call of God, and you must be aware of that so it comes as no surprise. You can be surrounded by hundreds of people and still feel alone.

Watchman Nee said this about loneliness:

> Loneliness is a mark of being an authority. All those who are frivolous among the brothers and sisters cannot be an authority. This is not pride. It merely means that for the sake of representing God's authority, we have to have certain limitations in our fellowship with the brothers and sisters. We cannot be too loose or easy-going. Sparrows fly in company, but the eagles fly alone. If we can only fly low and not suffer the loneliness of flying high, we are not qualified to be an authority. In order to be an authority, we have to be restricted and must separate ourselves. We cannot do what others can freely do. We cannot say what others can hastily say. We have to submit to the Spirit of the Lord. The Holy Spirit within us will teach us. This will make us lonely; it will strip us of excitement. We will no longer dare to joke around the brothers and sisters. This is the price that an authority has to pay. We must sanctify ourselves as the Lord Jesus did before we can be an authority.
>
> A servant of God is one who has God's holy ointment upon him. He must sacrifice his own emotion and abandon his legitimate sentiments. This is the only way to become a deputy authority. Anyone who maintains God's authority must also reject his own feeling. One must be willing to pay any price, even to the extent of giving up his deepest affections, his filial sentiments, his friendships,

and even his love. If he is entangled by these things, he cannot serve the Lord. God's requirements are strict. If a man does not give up his own affections, he cannot serve the Lord. God's servants are those with a distinction, while ordinary people are those without a distinction. God's servants must sanctify themselves for the sake of His people.[6]

When you say yes to the call of God upon your life, you have to understand it is a holy service. It's a life of consecration. A woman does not consecrate herself because she has chosen God, but God is the One who chooses us and then we turn around and consecrate our lives back to Him. It's not a favor we do for God or a courtesy to Him, but it is our way of giving back to Him for calling us into His service. Consecration is the result of being chosen. When God chooses you, you are called to live up to a higher standard than everyone around you. It cannot be looked at as a sacrifice but the highest honor in the entire world. Paul said those who have consecrated themselves to the Lord yield everything to Him:

> I beseech you therefore, brethren, by the mercies of God, that ye present your bodies a living sacrifice, holy, acceptable unto God, which is your reasonable service. (Romans 12:1)

How do you present your bodies a living sacrifice? By becoming consumed with the things of God and realizing everything in your life is for Christ Jesus and for Him alone. Those who understand the power of a consecrated life will allow themselves to become great vessels for the kingdom of God, and the anointing of the Holy Ghost will flow through them.

THE POWER OF A PURGED VESSEL

In the summer months, I enjoy getting outside and doing yard work. I get my clippers going, and every bush and tree on my property knows it's getting ready to get a good haircut. If you have ever had to clip or trim bushes and trees, you understand how irritating tree suckers can become. Tree suckers are the little sprouts and twigs that begin to grow from the side or root of a healthy tree trunk. They look so harmless and scrawny and are just a pain to deal with because they grow so fast. One week you cut them off; then the next week they are growing right back out of the trunk of that same tree.

But did you know that if those little, scrawny twigs are not removed and cut from that tree, they will eventually suck the life out of that healthy branch? A tree sucker will extract the energy and vitamins from the healthy part of that tree and steal the nutrients it needs to produce good fruit. Eventually, if they are not cut out of that tree, they will disfigure and hinder the growth of that branch.

Jesus passed on a powerful spiritual secret to His disciples when He taught them about cutting things out of tree branches:

> I am the true vine, and my Father is the husband-
> man. Every branch in me that beareth not fruit he
> taketh away: and every branch that beareth fruit,

he purgeth it, that it may bring forth more fruit. (John 15:1–2)

Most of the time, we read this passage and focus on the branch that is not bearing fruit, and we apply this to winning souls. However, John 15 has nothing to do with winning souls. Jesus was addressing the subject of His people loving each other and bearing the fruit of the Spirit in our lives. After Jesus discussed the branch that is not producing fruit, look at what He said about the good branch that is producing fruit:

> And every branch that beareth fruit, he purgeth it, that it may bring forth more fruit. (John 15:2)

The word *purge* means to "clean" or "He cleanses it." This means He cleans things out of that healthy branch that will hinder its growth. This branch Jesus is talking about is you and me. This branch is committed to God and serving the Lord. This branch is called of God. This branch has a relationship with God, but it is still in need of purging. Listen to what the Spirit is saying here! There will be times in our lives when we have to go through a purging process and get rid of some things.

There will be times we have to empty ourselves all over again and cleanse things out of our lives that may not be sin but are hindrances that cause blockage to our spirit. We have to look into the closed closets of our lives, pulling out drawers that we don't want to look in. We have to clean under the bed. I am not referring only to spiritual matters or things connected to your spiritual life, but I'm addressing things we allow into our lives in the physical realm. These things we have allowed to speak and attach themselves to us are literally consuming, little by little, the life and breath and nutrients out of everything God wants to do in our lives.

You can lay over an altar all day long and weep and cry and pray, then get up from that place of worship and refuse to recognize that carnal, worldly thing in your life that is attached to you as a *spirit sucker*—something that keeps you from advancing, growing, and maturing in God. It doesn't matter how many hours you pray in tongues; if you have outside voices (and I don't mean just human voices) speaking into your life in the form of entertainment, movies, pleasures of the flesh, comforts of certain types of music, and things of the world, they feed you and will eventually disfigure and rob you of the things God desires to grow and develop in your life.

Most of the time, the devil is not our biggest enemy; it's our flesh. And our flesh likes things that suck the life out of our spirit. It's easy to justify certain spirit suckers, easy to excuse them and commonly accept them as a part of our lives, but they can end up becoming the most damaging tool of destruction. There is nothing more powerful than a vessel who lives in pure honor to her Master and who keeps her vessel free from cracks, rocks, and impurities of the world that could cause the Master to reach for another vessel to use. The Potter's field is full of vessels that once sat in the hand of the master Potter, but because of some type of resistance, maybe some insignificant blemish it refused to release, that vessel was no longer available for use by the master Potter. That vessel, once chosen and dug from the earth, finds its way into the graveyard of broken dreams, cast into the open ditch of forgotten and forsaken ministries.

Have you been wondering why there has not been some great change, deep moves of God, or special visitations taking place in your life recently? Maybe you feel you have been in a dry desert and cannot understand why. Perhaps it's time for a purging in your life. If you really desire for God to be able to use you in the way He desires, you will go through certain seasons when God will call for a purging and emptying of your spiritual house, which is always connected with natural pleasures and things that are enjoyment to the flesh.

I remember my freshman year in Bible college. God had already done a miracle for me and made a way for me to come to Bible college, and I was in love with God and anxious to step with both feet into whatever He had for my life. I was in this thing for the long haul; I was serving God with everything in me—not holding anything back.

On our big class trip to San Francisco, three other friends and I piled in my car, and with windows rolled down and our hair blowing out the window down the highway, we sang our hearts out all the way into the city.

I had always loved Whitney Houston's music. I had several of her CDs (okay, this was before iPods), and on the way home that day I pulled out one of her CDs and popped it into the player. As we were cruising down Highway 101, giving a free concert to every car that passed us, singing, "I will always love you," I began to feel something I had never felt. It started deep in the pit of my soul, and I began to feel convicted over my Whitney Houston music. No one else in the car was feeling it. It's like Jesus just pulled the blinders back that day, at that moment in time, and let me see how much this "comfort music" was sucking something spiritual out of me. Jesus allowed me to feel the clash of the two spirit worlds that were trying to gain access into my life, and one of them had to go.

My friends probably thought I was the most fanatical nut when I popped that CD out of the player, placed it in the case, rolled down the window, and tossed it onto Highway 101. They didn't feel what I was feeling. I knew I had a call of God upon my life, and I could not do some of the things I used to do nor some things the others did. I didn't preach to them, and I didn't make them feel bad for listening to it, because this wasn't about anyone else in that car. I just had a great hunger to please God, and that afternoon I realized even the small things that stood in the way of that calling had to go. There was only one throne in my heart, and only one King could sit on that throne. That King refused to share His glory with any other.

Something took place in my life that day that caused me to turn a corner. I'm glad I listened to that voice. I'm glad God revealed that spirit sucker to me. That small choice made a difference in the way that I grew and the direction my life channeled. My friend, these things do make a difference! God will *try you* to see how serious you are about this thing. He will watch how you respond to temptations and small things that may seem insignificant and unimportant. He will see what you're willing to stand up for, stand up to, and stand against.

A vessel that mars itself with the residue of worldliness or a vessel that does not recognize and guard its usage but allows anything and everything to flow into it will be a vessel of dishonor in the hands of a holy God. Those vessels are the ones that end up in the Potter's field, vessels that become numb to the shame of sinful actions, or things the flesh desires. You have to consciously make an effort to keep your vessel protected and guarded from the stain and destruction of sin and worldly pleasures.

You see, God watches how much you're willing to give. He watches and takes notes of the things you allow into your life. He pays attention to the voices that you allow to speak into your spirit on a daily basis and where you place your boundaries. He watches how much or to what extent you're willing to cleanse and purge things from your life—things that may not be a sin but will be to you a spirit sucker that will hinder and block the flow of God's Spirit moving in your life. James said this:

> Therefore to him that knoweth to do good, and doeth it not, to him it is sin. (James 4:17)

As a woman who has a call of God upon her life and a desire for God to use her, you have to walk a consecrated lifestyle that rises above reproach on every level.

Joy Haney says this about the power of consecration:

> The prophets Elisha and Elijah were making one of their usual rounds, and while Elijah knew that his departure was soon to come, he told Elisha, "You stay here, for God is sending me to Bethel." Elisha answered and said, "As the LORD liveth, and as thy soul liveth, I will not leave thee." So they went to Bethel together.
>
> While in Bethel, again Elijah said, "You stay." And Elisha refused. Here is an important lesson to learn. A voice will say, "Park here," but you must watch where you park. While it is human to want to rest in a comfortable place, it may not be the will of God for you. You will have to learn how to discern when and where to park and when the will of God says to keep moving.
>
> The sons of the prophets at Jericho said, "Knowest thou that the LORD will take away thy master from thee?" But Elisha repeated the same answer to them, "Yea, I know it; hold ye your peace." Then, his leader Elijah said to him, "Tarry here, I pray thee; for the LORD hath sent me to Jordan." Again, Elisha looked at him and refused to stay behind when he said, "As the LORD liveth, and as thy soul liveth, I will not leave thee."
>
> Many people will join with the fifty prophets standing to view from afar, but only those who tenaciously stay close to Jesus and sell out completely to Him will see the miraculous. By the bank of the Jordan, suddenly Elijah reached over, grabbed his mantle, and smote the waters so they

divided, and the two men were able to walk on dry ground. Those who go the extra mile with God are always rewarded.

This is evident in Genesis 35, as Jacob was on his way back to Bethel. God had shown Himself strong by answering Jacob's prayer as He healed the relationship between him and his brother Esau. But now something even greater was getting ready to take place in Jacob's life as God prepared to change his name and pronounce the greatest blessing in the history of humankind upon him. Watch how God tested him first. Look at what had to happen before the release of blessing and promotion could come upon him.

> And God said unto Jacob, Arise, go up to Bethel, and dwell there: and make there an altar unto God, that appeared unto thee when thou fleddest from the face of Esau thy brother. Then Jacob said unto his household, and to all that were with him, *Put away the strange gods that are among you, and be clean, and change your garments:* and let us arise, and go up to Bethel; and I will make there an altar unto God, who answered me in the day of my distress, and was with me in the way which I went. And they gave unto Jacob all the strange gods which were in their hand, and all their earrings which were in their ears; and Jacob hid them under the oak which was by Shechem. (Genesis 35:1–4, my emphasis)

There had to be a purging of certain voices and influences in Jacob's life before this spiritual transition could take place. They had brought gods made with wood and stone that were more of a comfort to them than a deity, and these gods were handed down from their parents. These were "innocent" gods they had in their homes, gods they had grown up with. The Lord knew these voices and influences had to be removed first. The obstacles needed to be completely removed from their lives before God was willing to release His call, purpose, and power in Jacob's life.

The Bible says that Jacob buried them. This meant he had to purge himself and never return to retrieve them. Jacob had to get rid of certain things that were spiritual hindrances before God would reveal Himself to Jacob and change his name. We may not have gods in our lives that are made of stone and wood, but what about our gods of entertainment and comfort? Now, before you shut me out, I want to make it clear I am not referring to all forms of entertainment but much of it.

All you have to do is touch some screen, and you have access to anything and everything out there. My friend, if there is a call of God upon your life, I caution you to guard your heart by guarding your eyes. You have to get to the place where you are hungry enough for God that you are willing to place boundaries over your heart and guard your spirit from things that will keep God from fully revealing His power in your life. Yes, it does make a difference what you watch. Yes, it does make a difference what you feed your spirit.

Movies, Youtube videos, and other forms of worldly entertainment will suck the life and nutrients out of the spiritual things God is trying to pour into your life. They come may across as innocent and something that relaxes your mind, but beware of these voices that are being released into your spirit! Modern-day movies are not innocent anymore (if they ever were).

Brother J. T. Pugh made reference to the importance of how we spend our time:

> A man was bragging to a friend of his, who was a Nobel prize winner, talking about some type of television show. In bragging he told the man, "I haven't missed one of those shows this entire year—all three hundred of them!" The fellow turned to him and quietly said, "My friend, time is the coin of life. How is it that you would allow a fool to spend it for you?" Your time needs to be protected and you need to use good judgment at where you invest your time. It is the coin of life.

A couple years ago, after our annual Landmark conference, my husband and I went for a couple days to the city of Carmel to get some rest. The little bed-and-breakfast where we stayed delivered a *USA Today* newspaper, and one morning, as I began to scan the paper, I came across this article. They were producing a new *Poltergeist* movie that fall. In 1982, the original movie came out with a plot highlighting a little girl who was drawn to the television in the living room by dark spiritual forces that were controlling her. It has been suggested that many who watched this movie became demon possessed, and the movie has been called "the most cursed production of all times." In the interview with the director, the newspaper explained:

> Television is a conduit from the spirit world. But in 2015, the screens are bigger, packing more menace. And there are screens throughout the house. If you take a child's toy and put it in the hands of evil spirits, you get some very unfunny clowns.

Even the world understands the voices that flow from screens of televisions, phones, and entertainment devices are connected to the spirit world! Things you subject yourself to via media technology are feeding your spirit. God will not share His house with anything unclean or with the filth of the world. I understand not all venues of entertainment are unhealthy, but learning how to protect and guard your spirit from those that are is vital. Our vessels house a holy God, and it's up to us to keep our vessels clean and pure.

Brother Pugh went on to say this about the importance of keeping a pure house:

> When a man or woman ministers to a congregation or group of people, their spirits are released into that audience. Their spirit, not God's Spirit at first, but that person's spirit is met by the congregation's spirit and they talk to each other and communicate quietly as something inaudible takes place. That congregation's spirit judges that person and mentally makes the decision if that person is okay or not, if they are smart-alecky, or if they are kind. When they begin to speak, the Spirit of God comes and begins to blend with that minister's spirit as the spirit of the minister and the Spirit of God becomes one. This only happens if the minister is compatible with divine things and if they have that association. It is very important.

Remember, hungry people do things others don't understand. Hungry people are radical people. Hungry people are misunderstood when they draw lines in the sand and cut things out of their lives. Hungry people bury gods under trees, burn things, and silence voices in their lives in ways others will never be able to understand. The call of God will take you far away from the influences of this world. It will sometimes require you to cut ties with some people in your life, but as you give these things to God, you empty yourself out and His Spirit is poured in.

Something spiritual happens whenever you sacrifice and destroy negative influences!

Samuel was on a mission from God to anoint Saul as Israel's first king. After the anointing oil dripped from his forehead and the call of God was being birthed, God asked Saul to kill and destroy every man, woman, teenager, toddler, and infant among the Amalekites. He was also commanded to destroy all of their oxen, sheep, camels, and donkeys.

> Now go and attack Amalek, and utterly destroy all that they have, and do not spare them. But kill both man and woman, infant and nursing child, ox and sheep, camel and donkey. (I Samuel 15:3, NKJV)

You may look at this and say, "That is so cruel to kill all those innocent little children!" but these Amalekites were vicious enemies of God and had one purpose of existence: to exterminate Israel. These people were the first ones to attack the children of Israel once they crossed the Red Sea and escaped from Egypt. They passed on this hatred for God's people from generation to generation.

God exposed to Saul the things that had to be totally destroyed, just like He will expose and reveal things in our lives that have to be destroyed—even if they seem innocent. Listen to the voice of God in your life and don't make the mistake Saul did. Instead of taking God seriously, watch what he did:

> And Saul attacked the Amalekites, from Havilah all the way to Shur, which is east of Egypt. He also took Agag king of the Amalekites alive, and utterly destroyed all the people with the edge of the sword. But Saul and the people spared Agag and the best of the sheep, the oxen, the fatlings, the lambs, and all that was good, and were unwilling to utterly destroy them. But everything despised and worthless, that they utterly destroyed. (I Samuel 15 7–9, NKJV)

Saul spared the king that day. He kept alive just one little voice that he thought he could control. When God has a calling upon your life, there cannot be one living thing speaking into your life that's connected to this world. Everything that represented God's enemy had to be killed and destroyed.

Saul's course of life changed the day he spared the king. God turned to him through the prophet and said, "Because you have rejected the word of the LORD, He also has rejected you from being king. . . . The LORD has torn the kingdom of Israel from you today" (I Samuel 15:23, 28 NKJV).

When you are tempted to ask yourself, "Do these things really matter?" ask Saul.

Saul, did you ever dream you would end up here? You were the man God had chosen to raise up and rule His people, you were anointed and called, but now everything has been stripped from you—your calling, your ministry, and even your relationship with God.

All because he refused to silence a voice. All because he didn't murder an influence of the world. Don't tell Saul that the little things don't matter. If he could speak to you from the grave today, with tears and passion he would cry out, "Kill them all! Don't let any of them live! Don't mess around with the call of God! Don't think these things don't matter! They may look innocent now, but they will come back around to destroy you!"

Hungry people are serious people. Hungry people don't compromise. Hungry people are not afraid to draw lines in the sand. They are willing to cut things out of their lives. They are not afraid to burn things and silence voices of deception. But God manifests Himself to the hungry. He reveals His power and glory to the hungry. He births fruit in the lives of those who are hungry, but the hungry prove their hunger by what they are willing to sacrifice.

I know this is not a popular subject in this entertainment-controlled culture, but God will use you to the extent of what you're willing to sacrifice. You will be the one who will determine how far and deep you go in God by the choices you make on a personal level.

It's a *personal* commitment; you cannot wait for a friend or even a spouse to respond. This is something that is only between you and God. But it carries so much weight, it will dictate what road you will travel. Great eagles fly alone. Great lions hunt alone. Great men and women of God walk alone—alone with God. But one woman with God is always the majority.

Leonard Ravenhill, who wrote the book, *Why Revival Tarries* (which I deeply encourage you to purchase), was a man who could bring down the convicting power of God like few people could. His great anointing was birthed through his intense passion for prayer.

In 1994 right before his death, he received a number of requests from seminary students who wanted to come to see him for the sole purpose of having him lay his hands upon them in order to receive his "mantle." On his deathbed he turned to his son, and with a burdened heart he said: "Everybody wants to have my mantle, but nobody wants my sackcloth and ashes."

To the woman who carries a call of God upon your life, your generation doesn't need another pulpit filled with smoke and fancy light shows. The people of this world are crying out for something that is real. They are crying for someone who will become hungry for the deep anointing and allow God to channel through her the old-fashioned power of God. Don't cheat your generation of that opportunity; go be that person God is calling you to be: a powerful, anointed, consecrated, emptied vessel of honor that has poured herself out so God can display His power and glory in this generation.

6 | *The Traps of the Call*

If you have ever visited an archeology museum while in the Middle East, you know that pottery was everywhere. Just like our houses are filled with silverware, glasses, and items we use every day, ancient homes were filled with vessels made of clay pottery. The potter's house was their Wal-Mart. His workshop had to be a relatively large place to house a potter's wheel, a space for treading on the clay (actually smashing it with his feet), a kiln for firing—some commentaries say the skies in that area were darkened day and night from the constant black smoke—and a place for storing all the vessels he was preparing to sell.

But just around the corner of the potter's house resided the potter's field, where the clay pits were located. The potters back then didn't go to Hobby Lobby and purchase a package of premade clay, soft and smooth and pliable like a lump of play-dough. The potter had to dig this hard stuff out of the veins of the earth; clean all the rocks, sticks, and debris out of it; carry it into the potter's house so it could dry into a powdered form; and then add water to it so it would become moldable.

Once all the clay had been extracted, the potter's field became nothing more than veins of an open grave. It became a place to house dead things.

Its eerie, forgotten remains were full of deep trenches, dark pits, and large holes. It became nothing more than an open-air market where trash and debris were thrown. All the bodies of dogs, cats, and other animals that died in the streets were thrown into the potter's field and left there to rot. The potter's field—also known as *Akeldama,* "Field of Blood"—became Jerusalem's garbage dump, a place to dispose of anything dead or unclean. What once was a field that yielded the material to produce precious and valuable vessels was now a forsaken, stinking place.

But there is something else that occupied spaces in the potter's field. Among the bones of the decayed bodies, the screams of the fighting vultures, and the stench of rotting garbage lay the most pitiful sight of all: vessels that at one time resided in the potter's house but were discarded and thrown there because they would no longer be of any use to the potter. Misfits and mistakes occupied this place.

In this forsaken graveyard lay vessels whose clay had at one time been hand-dug by the potter. As he dug the chosen clay from the earth and carried it carefully into his house, he saw something in that clay that would one day make a mighty fine vessel for the potter's use. But somewhere in the making and forming of these vessels, something went wrong. The vessels that lay in this field were not tossed there on a whim or out of carelessness or impatience, but the potter once held these vessels in his own hands. There was a time in that vessel's life when the master potter had vision, dreams, and purpose for that vessel . . . but something in that vessel resisted the pressure, heat, and confinement of the spinning of the potter's wheel.

The Scriptures confirm that God refers to our lives as "vessels":

> But we have this treasure in earthen vessels, that the excellency of the power may be of God, and not of us. (II Corinthians 4:7)

> But in a great house there are not only vessels of gold and of silver, but also of wood and of earth; and some to honour, and some to dishonour. If a man therefore purge himself from these, he shall be a vessel unto honour, sanctified, and meet for the master's use, and prepared unto every good work. (II Timothy 2:20–21)

How do vessels that once were chosen by the potter as vessels of honor find themselves lying in the shadow of the potter's house, broken and forsaken in the potter's field? Take a walk with me through the potter's field. Every vessel that lies here has its story.

When you have a call of ministry upon your life, you better understand that you are walking around with a target on your back that is noticed by the spirit world. You will face things that others will not go through; you will walk through fires and wade through floods that others will never be touched with. And even though the calling will carry you through anything the enemy brings your way, you must be aware of the deceptive lures the enemy uses on the elite chosen of God because His purpose is to see you as a product of the potter's field rather than the potter's house.

Let's uncover and expose some of these techniques that are used in the hands of our enemy to bring harm to God's vessels. My prayer is for God to reveal things that can trip us and hinder our ability to become the vessel of honor He desires us to be.

SPIRITUAL PRIDE

I remember years ago hearing Brother Billy Cole, who was an apostle to Thailand and a powerful man of God, make the statement that spiritual pride will be the minister's greatest battle when God begins to use a person. It creeps into your spirit unaware and lures you through various avenues that seem so innocent, but behind the mask hides the ugly face of spiritual pride. First of all, let's talk about how destructive, powerful, and deceiving pride can be. Let's pull back the camouflage and take a deep and honest look at how pride creeps into our heart and how God responds to pride. I will be honest with you, after researching and digging into this subject, I had to a lot of repenting to do, and I asked God to help me become more aware of this evil lure that has been the destruction of so many powerful and effective men and women of God through the years.

Once Satan was cast to the earth, the spirit of pride inside him didn't waste any time before it destroyed its next victim. We all know the story of Eve and the forbidden fruit, but take a closer look at *what* tempted her and gave her the desire to eat it:

> For God doth know that in the day ye eat thereof, then your eyes shall be opened, and ye shall be as gods, knowing good and evil. (Genesis 3:5)

Something within Eve was not content just being a mortal human who walked with God. Instead, something lived inside her that wanted to be lifted up. She desired to be powerful and lifted up as a "god." The enemy coaxed and wooed her to follow her heart's feelings and desires, as he made it look so simple and innocent. He knew pride would be the downfall that would cause sin to enter the human race and destroy all hope for God's loving creation. After all, that is what caused his fall from Heaven.

Through the ages, in the lives of the men and women of the Scriptures, you can see pride raise its ugly head. If you live for God long enough and if God ever uses you to minister to others, it will come to you. You have the choice to recognize it and either tolerate it or make the decision to fight it. It's worth the fight! Over and over the Bible tells us about the destruction that is involved with those who allow pride in their lives:

> The fear of the LORD is to hate evil: pride, and arrogancy, and the evil way, and the froward mouth, do I hate. (Proverbs 8:13)

> Pride goeth before destruction, and an haughty spirit before a fall. (Proverbs 16:18)

The night of the Last Supper, the night before Jesus would go to the cross, His disciples were involved in a debate over which of them was the greatest.

> And there was also a strife among them, which of them should be accounted the greatest. And he said unto them, The kings of the Gentiles exercise lordship over them; and they that exercise authority upon them are called benefactors. But ye shall not be so: but he that is greatest among you, let him be as the younger; and he that is chief, as he that doth serve. (Luke 22:24–26)

Even though this debate was two thousand years ago, the conflict still lingers in the culture you and I are in. It will be there to trap ministers in the next generation if the Lord tarries His coming.

By the year 2000, around 100 million people had access to the Internet, and it became quite common for people to be engaged socially online. Of course, then it was looked at as an odd hobby and something new. Still, more and more people began to utilize chat rooms for making friends, dating, and discussing topics of their choice. But the huge boom of social media was still to come.

Back in the early 2000s the website myspace.com was the popular place to set up a profile and make friends. MySpace was the original social media profile website, leading into the world of websites like Facebook, Instagram, and Snapchat.

Social media hit the world with a bang, and unfortunately, it's here to stay. I understand there are a few positive points that social media delivers, such as staying in touch with family members, staying connected with friends who live afar, and advertising church events. At the same time, as a pastor's wife for over twenty years, I have watched social media flood our world, increasing feelings of insecurity and draining self-confidence in every corner of our lives.

Posts on social media try to present an idealized version of what's happening in a person's life, what something looks like, or how things are going. This can lead users to compare themselves constantly to others and to think less of their own lives. If things are going particularly well for people in your newsfeed and you're having a rough day, of course this will likely negatively affect your mood. In fact, in 2012 a team of researchers in the UK surveyed users, 53 percent of whom said social media had changed their behavior; 51 percent said the alteration was negative because of a decline in confidence they felt due to unfair comparisons to others.

Social media can lead to *fear of missing out* (FOMO). This is a phenomenon that occurs when you feel pressure to be doing what everyone else is doing, attend every event, and share every life experience. It can evoke anxiety and cause social media users to question why everyone is "having fun without them." Surveys have even found that people feel insecure after using Facebook and Twitter, which can produce negative thought patterns that make them infer they aren't successful or smart enough.

It starts out as a friendly dog that wags its tail and longs for you to pet it, but if you stick around too long and give it too much attention, it will eventually reach up and bite you. And we keep going back to the biting dog. Take a self-test: delete your social media apps or close your accounts, and take a break for a month or two. Experience for yourself the difference it makes in so many areas of your life. Knowing less is more. Paul understood this powerful secret of protecting his spirit when he wrote in I Corinthians 2:2:

> For I determined not to know any thing among you, save Jesus Christ, and him crucified. (I Corinthians 2:2)

Social media has also become an enormous pedestal for women who have callings upon their lives (and I'm addressing women because that is who this book is addressed to even though men are definitely entwined in this as well). Women can use the pulpit of social media to declare to the world *how* God is using them, *where* God is using them, how powerfully they ministered, *whom* they ministered with, what happened under "their" ministry, what names they were associating with, and the list goes on and on. I am honest enough to say that I have innocently done this in the past but God dealt with me about what this was producing in my spirit and I have tried to be careful since that time. It provides an undercover and deceiving platform for the spirit of pride to raise its ugly head.

Just because it seems like everyone is doing it does not mean it's right! Whatever happened to the spirit of humility that Jesus so emphatically taught over and over again to His disciples? What happened to, "Let nothing be done through selfish ambition or conceit, but in lowliness of mind let each esteem others better than himself" (Philippians 2:3, NKJV). Do we just toss those teachings into the "old-fashioned" corner? The enemy wants us to believe that just because it's prevalent in our culture that it's okay. Just because the staged world of social media is showing you everything they want you to see does not mean the Lord approves of these actions.

The Scriptures are always right; God's ways and methods are always right no matter what the culture or society is telling us. My friend, the power of God flows through humility. It's always been the pipeline His anointing flows through, and that is never going to change no matter who is bragging (yes, I did say that) on their abilities or taking pictures of themselves ministering or praying for people in the altar. We are in a "look at me" generation, but that does not change the fact that *God resists the proud* no matter what venue or podium you stand on to display it. Social media is a nameless, faceless voice that says so much about an individual through her actions, that I cannot hear what she is saying. A wise man once said:

> Let another man praise thee, and not thine own mouth; a stranger, and not thine own lips. (Proverbs 27:2)

If the two men who were told by Jesus to untie the colt for Him to ride on had lived in this generation, it would have been all over Twitter and Facebook with pictures of them standing next to the colt, testifying how God used them to fetch the colt for Jesus. Watch out for the trap of pride! When it is so important to you that everyone sees where you have been, where you have spoken, and how God is using you, recognize the enemy that is gaining territory on your heart.

For the sincere, godly woman that you are, I want to encourage you to listen to the Holy Ghost that speaks to you, not what the culture speaks or even what others are doing. John the Baptist, the greatest man of God who ever walked the earth according to the words of Jesus, understood the goal was to point men to Jesus when he wrote:

> He must increase, but I must decrease. (John 3:30)

All the new avenues that have become available for people to announce themselves and their ministry have become a proven and productive lure of the enemy to reel their souls into the waters of spiritual pride.

> Humble yourselves in the sight of the Lord, and he shall lift you up. (James 4:10)

If you will obey God, walk in the spirit of humility, and *allow Him* to broadcast your calling and ministry, the Lord will open doors for you that you never could have opened on your own. It's all about trust. It's all about having complete confidence in *Him* and trusting Him with every aspect of your ministry. The Lord takes notice every time you are tempted to post something that is gratifying to the flesh (we have all been there), but let your choice pass through the prayer filter of "Is it really unto Him?" With the flood of social media, there will be constant testing every time you open your phone or computer and see others who are blatantly exposing the things God said should be done in secret:

> Take heed that you do not do your charitable deeds before men, to be seen by them. Otherwise you have no reward from your Father in heaven. Therefore, when you do a charitable deed, do not sound a trumpet before you as the hypocrites do in the synagogues and in the streets, that they may have glory from men. Assuredly, I say to you, they have their reward. But when you do a charitable deed, do not let your left hand know what your right hand is doing, that your charitable deed may be in secret; and your Father who sees in secret will Himself reward you openly. (Matthew 6:1–4, NKJV)

Promoting yourself does not produce what the enemy makes you think; actually it is much the opposite. I recently had a friend, who is the Ladies Ministries president in her district, express to me there are certain speakers and ministers she will not invite to come to her district because of everything they expose of themselves on social media. Thinking that the self-exposure will open doors of ministry for them, they actually create the opposite response. It reminds me of the story of the "Emperor's New Clothes":

> Many years ago there was an emperor so exceedingly fond of new clothes that he spent all his money on being well dressed. He cared nothing except to show off his new clothes. In the great city where he lived, every day many strangers came to town, and among them one day came two swindlers. They

said they could weave the most magnificent fabrics imaginable. Not only were their colors and patterns uncommonly fine, but clothes made of this cloth had a wonderful way of becoming invisible to anyone who was unfit for his office, or who was unusually stupid.

Those would be just the clothes for me, thought the emperor. *If I wore them I would be able to discover which men in my empire are unfit for their posts. And I could tell the wise men from the fools. Yes, I certainly must get some of the stuff woven for me right away.* He paid the two swindlers a large sum of money to start work at once.

They set up two looms and pretended to weave, though there was nothing on the looms. All the finest silk and the purest old thread which they demanded went into their traveling bags, while they worked the empty looms far into the night.

I'd like to know how those weavers are getting on with the cloth, the emperor thought, but he felt slightly uncomfortable when he remembered that those who were unfit for their position would not be able to see the fabric. It couldn't have been that he doubted himself, yet he thought he'd rather send someone else to see how things were going.

"I'll send my honest old minister to the weavers," the Emperor decided. "He'll be the best one to tell me how the material looks, for he's a sensible man and no one does his duty better."

So the honest old minister went to the room where the two swindlers sat working away at their empty looms. *Heaven help me,* he thought as his eyes flew wide open, *I can't see anything at all.* But he did not say so. Both the swindlers begged him to be so kind as to come near to approve the excellent pattern, the beautiful colors. They pointed to the empty looms, and the poor old minister stared as hard as he dared. He couldn't see anything, because there was nothing to see. *Heaven have mercy,* he thought. *Can it be that I'm a fool? I'd have never guessed it, and not a soul must know. Am I unfit to be the minister? It would never do to let on that I can't see the cloth.*

"Don't hesitate to tell us what you think of it," said one of the weavers.

"Oh, it's beautiful—it's enchanting." The old minister peered through his spectacles. "Such a pattern, and what colors! I'll be sure to tell the emperor how delighted I am with it." "We're pleased to hear that," the swindlers said. They proceeded to name all the colors and to explain the intricate pattern. The old minister paid the closest attention, so that he could tell it all to the emperor. And so he did.

The emperor presently sent another trustworthy official to see how the work progressed and how soon it would be ready. The same thing happened to him that had happened to the minister. He looked and he looked, but as there was nothing to see in the looms, he couldn't see anything. "Isn't it a beautiful piece of goods?" the swindlers asked him, as they displayed and described their imaginary pattern.

I know I'm not stupid, the man thought, *so it must be that I'm unworthy of my good office. That's strange. I mustn't let anyone find it out, though.* So he praised the material he did not see. He declared he was delighted with the beautiful colors and the exquisite pattern. To the emperor he said, "It held me spellbound."

All the town was talking of this splendid cloth, and the emperor wanted to see it for himself while it was still in the looms. Attended by a band of chosen

men, among whom were his two old trusted officials—the ones who had been to the weavers—he set
out to see the two swindlers. He found them weaving
with might and main but without a thread in their
looms. "Magnificent," said the two officials already
duped. "Just look, Your Majesty, what colors! What
a design!" They pointed to the empty looms, each
supposing that the others could see the stuff.

What's this? thought the emperor. *I can't see
anything. This is terrible!*

*Am I a fool? Am I unfit to be the emperor? What
a thing to happen to me of all people!* "Oh! It's very
pretty," he said. "It has my highest approval."
And he nodded approbation at the empty looms.
Nothing could make him say that he couldn't see
anything. His whole retinue stared and stared. One
saw no more than another, but they all joined the
emperor in exclaiming, "Oh! It's very pretty." And
they advised him to wear clothes made of this wonderful cloth especially for the great procession he
was soon to lead. "Magnificent! Excellent! Unsur-
passed!" were bandied from mouth to mouth, and
everyone did his best to seem well pleased. The
emperor gave each of the swindlers a cross to wear
in his buttonhole, and the title of "Sir Weaver."

Before the procession the swindlers sat up all
night and burned more than six candles, to show
how busy they were finishing the emperor's new
clothes. They pretended to take the cloth off the
loom. They made cuts in the air with huge scissors.
And at last they said, "Now the emperor's new
clothes are ready for him."

Then the emperor himself came with his
noblest noblemen, and the swindlers each raised an
arm as if they were holding something. They said,
"These are the trousers, here's the coat, and this is

the mantle," naming each garment. "All of them are as light as a spider web. One would almost think he had nothing on, but that's what makes them so fine."

"Exactly," all the noblemen agreed, though they could see nothing, for there was nothing to see.

"If Your Imperial Majesty will condescend to take your clothes off," said the swindlers, "we will help you on with your new ones here in front of the long mirror."

The emperor undressed, and the swindlers pretended to put his new clothes on him, one garment after another. They took him around the waist and seemed to be fastening something—that was his train—as the emperor turned round and round before the looking glass.

"How well Your Majesty's new clothes look! Aren't they becoming!" he heard on all sides. "That pattern, so perfect! Those colors, so suitable! It is a magnificent outfit."

Then the minister of public processions announced: "Your Majesty's canopy is waiting outside."

"Well, I'm supposed to be ready," the emperor said and turned again for one last look in the mirror. "It is a remarkable fit, isn't it?" He seemed to regard his costume with the greatest interest.

The noblemen who were to carry his train stooped low and reached for the floor as if they were picking up his mantle. Then they pretended to lift and hold it high. They didn't dare admit they had nothing to hold. So off went the emperor in procession under his splendid canopy. Everyone in the streets and the windows said, "Oh, how fine are the emperor's new clothes! Don't they fit him to perfection? And see his long train!" Nobody would confess that he couldn't see anything, for that would prove him either unfit for his position or a fool. No costume the emperor had worn before was ever such a complete success.

"But he hasn't got anything on," a little child said.

"Did you ever hear such innocent prattle?" said his father. And one person whispered to another what the child had said, "He hasn't anything on. A child says he hasn't anything on."

"But he hasn't got anything on!" the whole town cried out at last.

The emperor shivered, for he suspected they were right. But he thought, *This procession has got to go on.* So he walked more proudly than ever, as his noblemen held high the train that wasn't there at all.

Spiritual pride works the same way in our lives. It wants us to think it lifts us to higher heights and deeper depths if we will only promote ourselves and our ministry. My husband always says, "Let God toot your horn."

That deceiving voice wants us to think that when we give in to its temptation and "toot our own horn," it will make everybody honor and respect us. The deceiving voice of pride will tell us it's all right because it will make us look important and will bring great esteem and recognition into our lives, when in reality, it will make us look spiritually immature, carnal, and lacking security in our relationship with God. In the end, the Scripture says that God resists the proud but gives grace to the humble. There is no amount of honor or esteem in this world that is worth being resisted by God! Remember this statement: It is not what others see, but it is what God knows.

The old saying, "Familiarity breeds contempt" is a message in itself.

Jesus made it clear to His disciples that whatever is done in secret will be rewarded openly:

> But you, when you pray, go into your room, and when you have shut your door, pray to your Father who is in the secret place; and your Father who sees in secret will reward you openly. (Matthew 6:6, NKJV)

As a leader and woman in ministry, this is something you will constantly have to fight, but it is definitely a fight worth having. Paul said that he died daily. How did he die? He didn't shoot himself every morning. He died to his image. He died to his pride. He died to his worthiness and to the competitive spirit that wanted to rise.

Donna Linville says this regarding the lure of social media:

> Much of social media feeds great insecurity in people. I read a statement regarding social media and the world of modeling. This statement said they airbrush and adjust the models to look however they want them to look through computer-generated abilities. They clear their skin, whiten their teeth, slim down their thighs, and brighten their eyes. It makes the youth dissatisfied with the natural. Social media is the same way. It's a staged environment that is causing a hype and rivalry that activates envy, jealousy, low self-esteem, and poor self-worth.

We must learn how to curb our appetites and use discipline in the areas that can hinder us. Discipline is recognizing and opening our hearts to what the Spirit is trying to say instead of being conformed to the expectations of the culture. The emphasis here is not intended to beat us down or make us feel guilty. Trust me, we have all made mistakes and been swept up with the desire to feel accepted, and I may be near the top of the list. We have all made choices that we regret. But today starts a new page in a chapter of your life, and small choices determine where we end up.

We have to look long and hard at these things that would be so much easier just to bypass and ignore while the enemy keeps his tackle box full of effective lures. I want to remind you that the subjects we are addressing are not written for just anybody but for the elite of God, those who are called with a holy calling and desire to live lives that are pure and consecrated to that call. This by far is one of the most powerful and most aggressive spirits a minister will wrestle with if God ever uses that person powerfully because the flesh is always at ought with the Spirit. There is constant war inside us that has to be fought through.

> For the flesh desires what is contrary to the Spirit, and the Spirit what is contrary to the flesh. They are in conflict with each other, so that you are not to do whatever you want. (Galatians 5:17, NIV)

Humility is not something we are born with or possess within our spirit naturally; it's something that can only be formed through the process of dying to our emotions, fears, and our plain, raw flesh. It is birthed through prayer and can only be fought through prayer. I pray Philippians chapter two over myself almost every single day—I actually have it printed on a piece of paper and taped to the wall in my prayer closet so I can be reminded day after day that this flesh of mine has to walk in a spirit of humility. And, trust me, it's a battle.

It's funny how it seems to be that one thing that keeps trying to crop up in my life. I expose it in prayer, lay it on the altar, deal with the issues going on inside my heart, and I feel good and free for about five days. Until that one thing literally grows legs, crawls off the altar, and somehow tries to gain entrance back into my heart. The enemy knows our weak points, and he will continue to sucker punch us in our weak areas. But what he doesn't know is the more we address these weaknesses and allow ourselves to become conformed to the cross, the stronger we will become!

Understand that it is God who will set the boundaries of your faith and ministry; it's not based on what others do. We live in a culture that is driven by success, but God's idea of success and our American idea of success are two completely different things. God says if you are obedient to what He has spoken to you, you are successful. If God tells you to teach the nursery kids each week and you do it out of obedience, you are just as successful as the person who prayed thousands through to the Holy Ghost last year. Just be obedient to the will of God, and be confident in the fact that it's not about what others see. It's about what God knows, and that is true success.

I remember speaking for a prominent church in our organization a few years ago, and after church, before I had to fly home, I wanted to get a picture with the pastor and his wife. Now, understand that these people were my dear friends for many years, and my motives were due to the fact that I truly loved them. I was sitting in the airport waiting on my flight when I thought I would just post that picture on my Instagram page. As I prepared to post it, the Holy Ghost, in a very small voice, spoke into my spirit not to post it.

Was there anything wrong with posting this picture? No. But that still, small voice began to caution me, and the choice was thrown in my lap at that moment. This was an inside test. No one would know that I felt this and probably no one would even think differently about the picture—but I knew. To be completely transparent, God knew this could be a way for the enemy to gain just a little bit of ground into my life through this small, insignificant outlet that would bring recognition to myself, and no one would know it but God and me. And it was all under the guise of ministry.

Thankfully, I listened to that voice (though some other times I have not).

Learning to listen to that still, small voice has kept me out of many dangerous places and helped me to protect my heart when I was not even sensitive to it myself. I can look back to that day and thank the

Lord that I did not post that picture—not because it was such a great sin—but because God was testing the ground of my heart and checking if He could trust me.

King Solomon once said:

> Above all else, guard your heart, for everything you do flows from it. (Proverbs 4:23, NIV)

God watches every time you take the low road. He sees every opportunity that comes knocking at your door as He steps back and watches how you respond to every opportunity spiritual pride has to slip inside. Remember this phrase that I have used several times throughout this book: *It's not what others see, but it's what God knows.* That's all that matters. A pure heart will become an empty channel for the Spirit of God to flow through, and humility will be the carrier of the anointing and a special place in God that can only be birthed when no one else sees.

Elsy Cunningham speaks on self-motivation:

> When you connect closely to the body of Christ, many times offenses will come, some from family members, and perhaps your husband. Some of the people you help the most may be the ones to hurt you the most. You cannot carry grudges from the day before. This is not easy for me to do, but it is a must. Being hurt deeply by someone you love and have even helped in the past will cause you to check your motives and ask, "Are you motivated by your own accolades or are you motivated by the Holy Spirit and building up the body of Christ?" Matthew 18:21–22 reminds us there are no limits to the number of times we must forgive.

Spiritual pride will come knocking on your front door, at every corner, and at every season of your life. I remember speaking at a conference with another speaker whom I had never met before that time. As the host of that conference took us out to eat, just in conversation this person began to tell me all the works she and her husband were doing, all the places she was traveling, and all the souls they had won. It all started out fine, and I sincerely rejoiced with her over the doors God had opened. But after a while, I could feel a slight tinge of intimidation starting to come upon me.

In my flesh, I wanted to combat her spiritual accomplishments with stories of my own spiritual accomplishments. My flesh just wanted to boot that spirit of humility I had been praying for right out the back door—but I felt a check in my spirit to keep my mouth closed. I felt God say, "Shhh."

Sometimes that is the hardest thing to do when everything inside you is screaming, "Look at me! I want to be valued too! Look at how involved I am in the Kingdom! I really am important also!" I think if we are honest with ourselves, certain people who come into our lives bring those feelings to life more than others. Don't get angry with the people, for they are only God's tools He uses to expose those things in our lives so we can get rid of things that will hinder us.

Brother Mark Morgan, who is my district superintendent, says it best:

> People are going to do you wrong, they are going to say stuff about you that is untrue and hurts,

but what are you going to do with it? Get bitter? Sit around and talk about them? It's just a test. Somebody has to crucify you because you cannot crucify yourself. Someone has to be used to crucify you and God sends these people as agents of crucifix. God sent them into your life. It's funny how Jesus called Peter His enemy and He called Judas His friend. Why? Because Peter was trying to stop Him from going to Calvary and Judas sent Him to Calvary. People who send you to Calvary to crucify you, they are not your enemy. They are the best friends you have because they are teaching you and developing in you the nature of Christ. Instead of talking about them, rejoice and thank the Lord for His agent of crucifix in your life because when it's all said and done, the love of God and the nature of Christ will be more manifest in you than ever before.

Have you ever cut a lemon in half and squeezed it into a glass of water, and all of a sudden seeds pop out and into the glass? You didn't see those seeds on the surface of the lemon, but as the juice got squeezed out of it, the seeds came out at the same time. It's the same way with our lives. God will use things (and most of the time it will be people) to squeeze things out of our lives that we don't even know are inside our hearts so He can use us.

I'm so glad I obeyed God that afternoon. I went back to my hotel room and talked to Jesus about what I was feeling and the intimidation I felt. Again reminded that the mark of spiritual maturity is the spirit of humility, and it is not always an easy path but is determined by actions. It is possible for a person to be filled with the Spirit of Christ but not possess the nature of Christ, for according to Philippians 2, the spirit of humility is the nature of Christ. As women of God, our entire purpose revolves around being conformed to the image of Christ. The road of humility involves crushing everything that makes you or your flesh feel important.

It's how you respond when you're in the heat of the battle and your emotions are screaming inside you, "Make me look great! Make me look spiritual! Make me look important." But Jesus is saying "Make yourself of no reputation and take upon the form of a servant." You make the choice by the actions you choose, and your response determines your growth and level of maturity.

Remember Romans 8:14, "As many as are led by the Spirit of God, they are the sons of God."

Claudette Walker addresses this subject:

> I do not feel restricted in any area of ministry as long as I stay in submission to my husband (who is my pastor), district superintendent, and general superintendent. I believe strongly in spiritual authority. I find my covering and protection in submission. If the Lord is truly leading you to an area of ministry, He will make it known to those over you, and you will not have to promote yourself.
>
> In Luke 14, Jesus told a parable that when we are invited to a wedding, we should willingly go and sit in the lowest room. He explained that if we take a seat in the highest room, we may be asked to move to the lower room when someone more honorable comes to the wedding.

And he put forth a parable to those which were bidden, when he marked how they chose out the chief rooms; saying unto them, When thou art bidden of any man to a wedding, sit not down in the highest room; lest a more honourable man than thou be bidden of him; and he that bade thee and him come and say to thee, Give this man place; and thou begin with shame to take the lowest room. But when thou art bidden, go and sit down in the lowest room; that when he that bade thee cometh, he may say unto thee, Friend, go up higher: then shalt thou have worship in the presence of them that sit at meat with thee. For whosoever exalteth himself shall be abased; and he that humbleth himself shall be exalted. (Luke 14:7–11)

In life, I try to prefer my brother or sister. It is such a safe and restful place to always take the lower position. This is true of our own opinions or positions in leadership.

Proverbs 27:2 says, "Let another man praise thee, and not thine own mouth; a stranger, and not thine own lips."

The world is screaming with its philosophy and its ads, self-esteem, self-promotion, self-actualization, and self-fulfillment! Does anyone notice a pattern? I have seen this world's philosophy of *self* bleed into the evangelical world. Lately, I fear the enemy is subtly causing it to bleed into our Apostolic ranks.

I simply cannot see Jesus or any of the apostles out promoting their own ministries. I know there is a subtle difference in offering tools and books to help the work of God progress, but that one verse stands as a huge stop sign to *self-promotion*. When the Lord called me, He told me never to try to open a door for my ministry but that He would be my door opener. I have stayed true to His directive, and He has kept His word to me. I personally do not want to stand in any pulpit God has not sent me to stand in and preach. As Pentecostals, we say we want to walk in the Spirit, yet so often we find ourselves involved with self-directed missions. I have a testimony that God is faithful. If you are willing not to promote yourself, you will open the door for God to promote you. He is a master at finding a shepherd boy singing to sheep on the hillside and anointing him to be king.

Someone reading this book may feel as if she is at a disadvantage because her family is not in ministry and she feels no one knows her. Dear lady, *He knows you!* You may be hidden in some dungeon now due to betrayal as Joseph was, but that God-given gift will rise to the surface and bring you before great men. I will share with you a test I give my spirit often. When others praise me or my gifts in sincere appreciation, I check my spirit. If I am enjoying it too much, an alarm goes off. If, however, when the words of praise come, my spirit is saying to the Lord, "Jesus, all this praise I now give to You, Lord," I know I am okay.

When the Lord has spoken His word through me and people have been touched and transformed by the power of God, often they give praise to me because I was the vessel God used to deliver His message. They say things like, "You are awesome," and other words of encouragement that are sometimes awkward to receive. The Lord trained me on how to handle their well-meaning expressions. I simply receive the hug. I smile when I hear their words of praise. I look in wonder at their beautiful smiles. Then I go back to my hotel room and say to the Lord, "Did You feel all their hugs, Jesus? Did You hear how awesome they think You are? Did You feel how very much they love *You?* Did You hear how much they treasure *Your words?* Jesus, those folks are crazy about You! I now transfer all their kind expressions of love from my spirit to Your Spirit because You alone are worthy of all praise and glory and honor, my Lord!"

That is my prayer of safety. The danger is in believing the words of praise and allowing the insidious spirit of pride to enter our hearts. We must daily seek the Lord and not allow a spiritual work to be done either motivated or carried through by our own selfish flesh. God is a jealous God, and His glory He will not give to another!

THE CONTROVERSY OF AUTHORITY

It's no secret that the world you and I are living in is vastly changing. Mentalities that have held families and marriages together in the past are now mocked, methods and teachings that are biblically sound are categorized as "old-fashioned," and methods that were made for our "protection" are now labeled as "oppression." We see the family unit being torn apart by worldly mentalities implementing modern techniques that do no more than feed the appetite of a dark spirit world and dig us deeper into pits of despair and destruction.

The spirit of Jezebel has raised its ugly head again in recent years. The Lord cautioned His church regarding Jezebel:

> Notwithstanding I have a few things against thee, because thou sufferest that woman Jezebel, which calleth herself a prophetess, to teach and to seduce my servants to commit fornication, and to eat things sacrificed unto idols. (Revelation 2:20)

The Barnes Commentary states this regarding Jezebel:

> Jezebel was the wife of Ahab; a woman of vast influence over her husband—an influence which was uniformly exerted for evil. She was a daughter of Ethbaal, king of Tyre and Sidon, and lived about 918 years before Christ. She was an idolater, and induced her weak husband not only to connive at her introducing the worship of her native idols, but to become an idolater himself, and to use all the means in his power to establish the worship of idols instead of the worship of the true God. She was highly gifted, persuasive, and artful; was resolute in the accomplishment of her purposes; ambitious of extending and perpetuating her power, and unscrupulous in the means which she employed to execute her designs.

Jezebel's main mission was to kill off the prophets of God. We can see how that spirit is prevalent in America; it's an evil spirit sent straight from Satan to destroy the family unit, our marriages, and the church. This spirit also engulfs an antichrist spirit, which is a spirit that refuses to be under any type of authority and breathes rebellion in all forms.

We recognize this uprising in the spirit world through the feminist movement that is prevalent in our culture. This movement is not just about human rights and equality, or a modern social movement, but it comes from ancient elements founded in the spirit of witchcraft and rebellion—the same spirit that was manifest years ago in Jezebel. We see it exposed through modern society by women who no longer want to be "tied down" by motherhood or feminine functions in the home, which goes directly against the command of God, written by the apostle Paul to Timothy:

> I will therefore that the younger women marry, *bear children,* guide the house, give none occasion to the adversary to speak reproachfully. (I Timothy 5:14, my emphasis)

> To be discreet, chaste, *keepers at home,* good, *obedient to their own husbands,* that the word of God be not blasphemed. (Titus 2:5, my emphasis)

We live in a culture where there is great animosity against God-ordained authority, and rebellion is the channel used to expose it. Do you know whom the spirit of Jezebel hates the most? Preachers who are not afraid to preach and declare the truth of God's Word and operate within the bounds of God-ordained authority. This spirit understands that a person who operates under the channel of proper authority can be powerfully used by God, and that is why it tries to introduce a spirit of rebellion.

Anytime a prevalent spirit is loosed upon the earth, you better believe that spirit will try to make its way into the church. A woman of God who feels a call to ministry must be aware of this spirit. We see the influence of this spirit all around us. The subject of authority goes against the streams of our society and godless culture, and our thinking patterns are influenced by this world's mentality more than we may realize. That is why we need to go back to the beginning and take a close look at how God intended things to run.

THE ORDER OF CREATION

One of the oldest traps the enemy can get a woman of God ensnared with is a desire to rule or be in charge. It was part of the curse that was placed upon the woman after the fall. In the beginning of Creation, God designed someone to be "the head" and He designed someone to be "a helper." Someone was appointed to be the provider and someone was designed to work beside that provider in his purpose. Let's look at this in the Scriptures:

> And the LORD God took the man, and put him into the garden of Eden to dress it and to keep it. (Genesis 2:15)

God created Adam first.

God commanded Adam to dress and to keep the garden before Eve ever came along. God instructed Adam on exactly what his responsibilities were: to guard the land that he was put in charge of and make it productive:

> And the LORD God commanded the man, saying, Of every tree of the garden thou mayest freely eat: but of the tree of the knowledge of good and evil, thou shalt not eat of it: for in the day that thou eatest thereof thou shalt surely die. (Genesis 2:16–17)

Second, God gave Adam spiritual responsibilities. Adam's responsibility was to be obedient to God and to set God's boundaries within his home. Adam knew the do's and don'ts of the garden. He was the one God ordained to be the spiritual authority in that soon-to-be marriage. Adam was the one who was responsible to teach his wife what God had said. From the beginning, it has been God's will for the man to be the spiritual leader in the home.

> And the LORD God said, It is not good that the man should be alone; I will make him an help meet for him. (Genesis 2:18)

Eve was created by God to be a complement to Adam and to work beside him in his calling. It was not about one lording over the other, but each had different and distinct roles he and she were to fulfill in that union.

Adam and Eve worked together, and everything was grand and glorious in the garden until sin entered into the world and affected their marriage and relationship. Before sin entered the world, Eve never had a problem with Adam being in authority or that

God instituted him to be the spiritual authority in the home. However, when sin entered their world, instead of complementing each other, they began to compete against each other.

God cursed the serpent first in Genesis 3:14; then He turned to the woman and pronounced this curse upon her:

I will greatly multiply thy sorrow and thy conception; in sorrow thou shalt bring forth children; and thy desire shall be to thy husband, and he shall rule over thee. (Genesis 3:16)

The battle of the sexes began when God turned to Eve and said, "Thy desire shall be to thy husband, and he shall rule over thee." In the original Hebrew, the phrase, "Your desire shall be for your husband," is translated (paraphrased) "the woman would now desire to dominate her husband" who was assigned by God to rule over her. Since they were created equally in the beginning, the woman probably had as much right to rule as the man did, but after the Fall, she was required to come under submission to her husband.

The New English Translation renders Genesis 3:16 this way:

> I will greatly increase your labor pains;
> with pain you will give birth to children.
> You will want to control your husband,
> but he will dominate you.

Now Eve had something she had to battle on a daily basis. Being submissive to her husband was not something that would come naturally to her or even be a natural desire. It would now be a source of conflict as those feelings of wanting to dominate or be in control were not there before the Fall. Now the woman has to fight her emotions and will to *submit herself* to the man in her life.

This helps us to understand why many women hate this authority issue so much. The feminist movement has become so forceful and militant in their cause because that old spirit of rebellion wants to override God's laws. God warned us ladies that being under authority was something we would at times struggle with, and that old spirit of the world wants to arise and defy God through challenging the human authority He has placed in our lives.

Claudette Walker makes this statement regarding authority:

> Let me first talk to any single lady ministers. My husband, Marvin, and I have taught single young men and women for years. We understand that, next to your decision to serve the Lord, your choice of a spouse is your second greatest decision. A woman who is called to ministry and chooses to marry must have a husband who sees her calling, believes in it, and is very secure in his own place in the Lord's kingdom.
>
> I have stood by and watched called, anointed young women marry the wrong people and never become everything God called them to be because they did not marry God's chosen husbands for them. This is a serious subject, but it is a revelation the Lord gave me. Proverbs 6:27:
>
>> Can a man take fire in his bosom, and his clothes not be burned?

This is referring to the fire of lust and an encounter with a whore or an adulteress. However, one day I was praying and the Lord showed me a young lady who had a fiery anointing from the Lord. It was like a raging fire in her bosom coming from her God-called and anointed heart. I saw her in the arms of a good man—he was Apostolic and faithful but not the man the Lord had chosen for her. He was insecure and very jealous of her calling; therefore, the fiery anointing in her heart would consume him. The two choices were sad. She could pursue her calling and watch her husband slowly melt away in deep insecurities, or she could lay her calling aside to try not to offend him. Either choice would lead to a very sad life. Saddest of all is: the part of the Kingdom she was called to build would be left neglected due to her marrying wrong.

My husband saw the call and anointing of the Lord upon me before I was brave enough to step out and walk in that call myself. Because my husband is so secure in the Lord and in who he is in God, jealousy has never been an issue in our marriage and ministries. When I would say, "I don't have anything to say!" he would tell me that I should pray and that God would give me His words. From my youth I have dealt with health challenges. When I think I should just stay home and not push past the pain and weakness, he encourages me, telling me I am called and must do what God asked me to do in spite of the weakness. He does all he can around our home to help me. He is my number-one intercessor when I minister. He is my safe place when I am discouraged, and I would never have been able to walk through all the doors the Lord has opened for me if I had not married the husband the Lord chose for me.

There are some wrong choices you can live with, but for a called and anointed lady in ministry, the decision to marry anyone other than God's choice has sad results regarding your own personal happiness. Even worse, the Kingdom's destinies are never achieved fully in your life. I know many of you are lonely, but remember there is no greater loneliness for a lady in ministry than having married wrong. Marvin and I have taught marriage seminars and conducted marriage counseling all over the world for close to forty years now. I said all that to say this: Single young lady in ministry, go on a God hunt not a man hunt!

Abraham sent his servant to find a wife for his son, Isaac. I love the prayer he prayed, and I prayed this same prayer for years for my only son:

> Now let it be that the girl to whom I say, "Please, let down your jar so that I may [have a] drink," and she replies, "Drink, and I will also give your camels water to drink"—may she be the one whom You have selected [as a wife] for Your servant Isaac; and by this I will know that You have shown lovingkindness (faithfulness) to my master. (Genesis 24:14, *The Amplified Bible*)

The Lord gave me a message called "Pacify Me or Crucify Me." It deals with pride versus humility. In the study, the Lord taught me not just to read Philippians 2:5–8 but to pray it:

> Have this same attitude in yourselves which was in Christ Jesus [look to Him as your example in selfless humility], who, although He existed in the form and unchanging essence of God [as One with Him, possessing

the fullness of all the divine attributes—
the entire nature of deity], did not regard
equality with God a thing to be grasped or
asserted [as if He did not already possess it,
or was afraid of losing it]; but emptied Himself [without renouncing or diminishing His
deity, but only temporarily giving up the outward expression of divine equality and His
rightful dignity] by assuming the form of a
bond-servant, and being made in the likeness
of men [He became completely human but
was without sin, being fully God and fully
man]. After He was found in [terms of His]
outward appearance as a man [for a divine-
ly-appointed time], He humbled Himself
[still further] by becoming obedient [to the
Father] to the point of death, even death on a
cross. (Philippians 2:5–8, *The Amplified Bible*)

When I pray on the armor of God, I pray this
way over my mind according to these verses.

Lord, You said that the same mind that was in
You should be in me also. So today I am asking
You to help me to make myself of no reputation.
Let me not be concerned with what others think
of me. Just as You made Yourself of no reputation,
today I want to think as You did. You were always
pointing the crowds to the work of the Father.
You said You could do nothing of Yourself. I want
to be concerned about the glory and honor of the
Lord, not my own honor. You took upon Yourself
the form of a servant, or a slave. Today, let me do
what You want me to do, *when* You want me to do
it, and *for as long as You ask* me to do it, and may I
do Your will with the same humble attitude You
displayed. You died to Yourself in Gethsemane

until You were willing to carry Your cross and die on it. Today, give me grace to carry my cross and die to my own ideas and will just as You did for me. Just as You did, Lord, today I willingly strip myself of all privileges and advantages and rightful dignity. Lord, today may this mind-set You lived by become my mind-set. Warn me when I am off base and set me on track, forgiving me my own carnal ways. I pray in Jesus' name for Your mind to be in me today, Jesus.

If you can only pray one short prayer a day, pray this one. You will have a built-in alarm system against adamic pride and a daily incentive to be yoked with the meek and lowly Jesus, living in submission to your husband and to God. At prayer meetings in Odessa, Texas, every morning, Brother J. T. Pugh would pray this prayer, "Save me from myself, Jesus!" As a twenty-three-year-old woman, I used to wonder what in the world he was talking about. I thought I needed to be saved from the world and the devil's schemes, but as I matured and encountered my own unregenerate, willful human nature, I joined Brother Pugh's daily and desperate plea, "Save me from myself, Jesus!"

More than anything else in my life, along with the fasting and prayer, this teaching led me to hate pride and to embrace humility. Since we are to be under the headship of our husbands, we constantly need to check our spirits and ask this question, "Why do I want to do this ministry? Am I answering a divine directive, or is this my flesh?" I have heard it stated that "not every good idea is a God idea." My simple desire in life is to stand before the Lord someday and hear Him say, "Well done, thou good and faithful servant." Submission to my husband and

196 | For Women Who Are Called by Women Who Have Answered

to those in authority over me is not difficult when I
realize He is protecting me, not restricting me.

Elsy Cunningham talks about the importance of
authority:

A great hindrance to a married woman of God is
when she has her own agenda. She needs to be
in sync with her husband's agenda and help him
accomplish the dreams that they, as a team, set out
to accomplish. It is sure to end in disaster when a
minister's wife sets out with the motive of seeking
prominence for herself. An attribute a minister's
wife must possess is flexibility, especially in her
schedule. If a minister's wife is so structured in
her schedule that she cannot handle change at a
moment's notice when her husband needs her, life
will be chaotic and end in disaster.

There are many ways a wife can minister to
her husband, and each family should develop its
own dynamic and learn to work together. Ministry is teamwork and can require the wife to
become a "buffer" for her husband. As a buffer,
I provide love to the church people, and in this
way I help them to better understand decisions
my husband (their pastor) makes that they may
not otherwise comprehend.

God will use you to minister to your husband by knowing his weaknesses and using your
strengths to uplift him. Realize your weaknesses,
work on them, and help your husband work on
his. I learned to identify strengths and weaknesses
through studying temperaments and gift analysis
materials, which have helped.

My husband's grandfather once told me that I
would be my husband's poorest boss but his best

advisor. Submission is not being a doormat; it is when you disagree but you ask the Lord to help you to submit. In reality, this is a broad subject with many variables. At times, my husband has pondered the things that I have said during an attack of the enemy and realized that the Lord was using me to speak to him. It all must be done in the right spirit, and God will honor it.

My husband and I were speaking at a ministers' conference in Oklahoma, and during a "heart to heart" panel discussion, the subject of authority was addressed. The question was, "Is there anything that can help us transcend the mind-sets that hold us back so we can walk in the next dimension of the Spirit?"

Charles Robinette, who is a missionary to Austria and other German-speaking countries, was one of the panelists that day, and he shared the most touching story, one I will never forget. I received his permission to share this with you:

> I was raised by a great pastor who always encouraged the young men in the church to pray and get hold of the Spirit of God, so when I came into the church as a teenager, that's all I knew. I would lay on the floor and speak in tongues, I would get lost in the Spirit as my parents would carry me home speaking in tongues until I woke up in the morning speaking in tongues. I learned to pray by my pastor's training.
>
> I can remember when I first left the military and came back home. I knew I was called of God. I came back from the military asking God to position me to the place I could walk in the Spirit and operate in the supernatural. I yearned to understand how

to operate in the Spirit to where many could receive the Holy Ghost at one time. Brother Billy Cole, an apostle to Thailand and a great man of God, had a vision of me one day. The Lord spoke to him to call my pastor and tell him that I was supposed to go to Ethiopia with him on the next crusade. I didn't know Billy Cole at the time, but he had a vision of me and I was supposed to come with him.

The trip was the most life-changing event for me. I was in the service where over one hundred thousand people received the Holy Ghost in one service, and there were so many people we could not see the back of the crowd. I was just a nobody from nowhere, a young man who had no ministry; I had never done anything for God. I was walking up to my hotel room when Billy Cole shouted from the stairwell, "Robinette, don't even go to your room. You're going to the youth crusade, and everybody will receive the Holy Ghost." I begged him not to make me go. I told him I was not a preacher and didn't even bring a Bible. Well, he just laughed and said, "The Lord will speak one Scripture to your mind, you will speak the word of faith, and all will receive the Holy Ghost." That night seven hundred people got the Holy Ghost, and it had nothing to do with me.

God put mighty men in my life and allowed me to see and witness things, but I also learned if you really want to be used of God, you sometimes have to change your circle of friends. *Don't talk about yourself* if you want to be used of God. When you're in a place where there are mighty men or women of God, don't talk about yourself. Just be quiet and let them speak, and be a sponge to what they're saying. Something will be imparted to you and you will be transformed.

I saw major transformations in my ministry by this little thing called radical submission. Submission is not a popular subject because people don't like the thought of being submitted, and they don't want people telling them what to do. If you ever want to be radically used of God and radically transformed by God, you have to become radically submitted to a man or woman of God who can literally say "no" and you obey.

I remember when my wife and I were leaving the military and we were scheduled to go immediately into the Secret Service branch. We had everything lined up and had an open door to go to Washington. I called my pastor and met with him, telling him that the next day I would be leaving for Washington to be in the Secret Service. He looked at me and said, "No, you're not. You're coming back to be my youth leader. Show up tomorrow morning at 10 AM, and I will tell you what your job will be." After that he got up and walked out of the restaurant. There was no discussion, there was no debate, and there was no compromising, nothing.

It was a test. It was a moment in time where my life was either going to be transformed or destroyed. I would have never gone to Ethiopia and experienced all I did if I had not radically submitted myself to the man of God in my life. I didn't know what to do; I just called up the Secret Service division and told them I was not coming. I showed up at the church the next morning at 10 AM, and six months later I went to Ethiopia. All of that was birthed in a moment of radical submission where I said, "Not my will, but Thy will be done." I don't understand this, I can't comprehend the reasoning, it doesn't fit in my plans, but the man of God in my life has spoken and that is good enough for me.

> I can remember from that time forth God began to transform my ministry; things began to happen and doors began to open for me.

Sometimes it's not an easy thing to submit to authority, especially when you know you're right. But sometimes God watches to see if you are willing to stay under His authority even when everything inside you is screaming against it. Eve was formed by God to be a "help meet" to Adam. She was never intended to lead the family or to make the final decisions in the home, but she was created to support and stand beside the man. The world tries to paint a dim picture of the word *submission,* but take a step back and look at all the dysfunctional marriages and messed-up family units. Don't talk of "equal rights" and "equality" and try to convince me of my rights as a woman when that world is a complete shipwreck. I want to do things God's way. I want to live under the protection not only of my husband but ultimately under God.

Claudette Walker makes this statement about the power of submission:

> A few years ago, Kim Haney asked me to speak at the Ladies' Advance conference in Stockton, California. Through her kindness and our friendship, I had ministered at several of the ladies' meetings there through the years. Kim Haney is my friend, and I love the freedom of worship and the connection I have in the Spirit with the precious ladies of Christian Life Center. I was hoping the calendar was free.
>
> As always, I consulted with my husband. He looked at his calendar and told me that weekend

was also scheduled for Michigan Mantle, which was a brand-new ministry my husband leads, where we, along with several other ministers, mentor young ministry couples from Michigan. For years my husband was a part of the Jonathan Project and was able to help mentor over a hundred young ministry families. When that ministry came to an end, he prayed for an open door to keep reaching out to young ministry families, for it is a calling from God and a passion of his. I stood at the island in our kitchen holding the calendar. To me, there was no choice to make. Without one prayer or hesitation, I called Kim and told her I would not be able to come since I would be mentoring young ministers' wives in a brand-new ministry my husband had started in Michigan.

I am speaking now to all of you lady ministers who are married to preachers. For me, that one schedule conflict was resolved by the godly principle of submission to my husband. *First and foremost my calling is to be a support to my husband in his calling.* I do not think of it as *my ministry* or how to promote or build it. My husband and I are *one,* and our ministries and callings are intertwined. Alarm bells should start to ring if you ever feel yourself desiring to promote your own ministry above your husband's calling. Although I obviously believe and know through experience that the Lord will call and anoint a female, I also know that my place is first and foremost at my husband's side as a help meet to his calling! *We must be very careful lest the insidious spirit of feminism that is so alive and active in the secular world seep into our hearts and ministries!* I feel so safe and protected under my husband's authority. If he feels a check in his spirit that I should not accept an invitation to preach, I do not go. I know that he loves me and is seeking not only to give me the freedom to obey the Lord's call but that he is watching out for my spiritual health and my emotional well-being. I have often told him that I really wish I could clone him. I have no idea why I was chosen to have the best husband God ever made, but I am eternally grateful!

Joy Haney talks about a woman's place in ministry:

It is a privilege when God raises up a woman and puts a call to the ministry on her life. He sees something in her that can be useful to His kingdom. Such was the case of Deborah the prophetess, who dedicated her life to God and did heroic deeds with a bold faith, which inspired the people over which she ruled as judge. She not only was the fifth judge of Israel but was a wife, a warrior, and a poetess. She composed a song which is regarded as one of the finest of ancient Hebrew poetry. This song of praise is found in Judges 5. Many theologians feel that her husband, Lapidoth, was in his quieter way the encourager of Deborah in all the roles that God asked her to fill. It is believed that in the home, she was submissive to her husband: the strong, quiet one, because God, who set up this order of authority, blessed her in every way. God blesses those who obey Him.

Biblical women are an example for this generation to follow, for those whom God used were all under authority or submissive to the authority figure God placed in their lives. Esther, the queen, was submissive to Mordecai. When her parents died, she came under the guardian care of Mordecai, a palace official, to whom she was related by marriage. She was always obedient to her elder cousin and, even when she became queen, sought his practical advice.

When Jesus was on earth, He showed by example that He had respect for women, and because of His attitude and reverence toward them, they were prominent in the activities of the early church. Women ministered to the apostles of their substance and became powerful helpers to Paul and the early work. In the case of Aquila and Priscilla, Paul wrote to the church that was at Corinth: "Aquila and Priscilla salute you much in the Lord, with the church that is in their house" (I Corinthians 16:19). Even though Priscilla was a strong personality who ministered with her husband, she was *under the authority* of her husband.

In Romans 16, Paul commended Phebe, a servant of the church who ministered to and helped many, and listed others: Mary, Julia, and again, Priscilla. Lydia is mentioned in the Book of Acts, as well as Philip the evangelist's four daughters who prophesied. God used many women for His purposes throughout the Bible. All the women whom God raised up who were recorded in the Scriptures did their job well, kept their femininity, and stayed in the order of authority that God instituted.

A woman in ministry should always keep her femininity and identity as a lady. The beloved disciple addressed one of his letters to "the elect lady" (II John 1). It should not make a woman *mannish*. God made you to be His representative of the feminine gender. Be the best you can to help make that distinction, and don't take on the mannerisms of a man.

It is important for a woman to be under authority as God instituted. If called to the ministry, she must be under subjection to her pastor and also her husband if she is married. When God calls someone, He equips her with what she needs. He will give you grace and favor to do His will without you usurping authority or disobeying whom God has put over you. Yes, we are all created equal! And the level of authority doesn't make anyone more important than the other. The priority of creation gave Adam headship but not superiority. All are important in God's kingdom. Everyone in his or her place submits to God's order: He set it up. God first, man second, and woman under the man. It's wonderful that God was protecting the woman in His great scheme of things in the home and in the church.

Submission never imprisons you. It liberates you, giving you the freedom to be creative under the protection of divinely appointed authority. Submission never means that your personality, abilities, talents, or individuality are buried, but that they will be channeled to operate to the maximum.

Matthew Henry says it well:

> If man is the head, she [woman] is the crown, a crown to her husband, the crown of the visible creation. The man was dust refined, but the woman was double-refined, one remove further from the earth. . . . The woman was *made of a rib out of the side of Adam;* not made out of his head to rule over him, nor out of his feet to be trampled upon by him, but out of his side to be equal with him, under his arm to be protected, and near his heart to be beloved.

If God has called a lady to minister, and she thinks she knows more than the pastor, she should keep that to herself and not talk about it to anyone. Obey God, submit, and let God open the doors for you to minister. Stay humble, and God will allow you to minister where He sees fit. "Humble yourselves therefore under the mighty hand of God, that he may exalt you in due time" (I Peter 5:6). Let God choose your audience to whom you will minister. Always let God guide your footsteps where He wants you to minister. And when He opens a door, walk through it with the blessing of the authority figure God has placed in your life.

My late husband, Bishop Kenneth Haney, had many friends in the Apostolic Spanish organization. I remember my first time to speak at one of the Apostolic Spanish conferences, and when they announced me, they brought a smaller pulpit to the floor for me to use. It was their custom for the women not to go on the platform. It was all right with me because it wasn't about me; it was about the Lord and His kingdom. I was an ambassador for Christ (I Corinthians 5:20), and my mission was to speak the words that He gave me in prayer. It didn't matter if I was on the platform or not. You see, to be used of God makes you a "servant" unto the Lord, as stated in several references:

Paul, a servant of Jesus Christ. (Romans 1:1)

James, a servant of God and of the Lord Jesus Christ. (James 1:1)

Simon Peter, a servant and an apostle of Jesus Christ. (II Peter 1:1)

Jude, the servant of Jesus Christ. (Jude 1:1)

I heard one preacher say, "Servants have no rights," but God's servants obey their Master and make Him look good. Women in ministry need to walk humbly before the Lord and do His bidding. Being in ministry is not trying to build your own name or become somebody. God forbid! It's about ministering to the hurting, helping set the captive free, sharing the precious Word of God so others might know Him and be set free.

Ministry is not glamorous; it is selfless giving of one's self to the greater cause of Christ's kingdom. It is praying daily, fasting often, learning of Him, and studying His Word, becoming more and more like Jesus and drawing nearer to God so others will see Him and not you when you speak and minister. They will know that you have been with Jesus, as was said about the disciples: "They took knowledge of them, that they had been with Jesus" (Acts 4:13). People know if it's about you or about Him. It bleeds through whatever you're doing. They feel the anointing and the authority in God. If He calls you, treat the call with reverence. Don't treat it lightly. It's a sacred thing to receive a call from God to work in His kingdom. Seek always to walk softly before Him, pleasing Him and giving your best to whatever He asks you to do. The main thing is to *please God* in everything you do, no matter what.

GUARDING YOUR APOSTOLIC IDENTITY

Every culture and generation has its challenges and methods of opposition that come against the church and its identity. These attacks are nothing new, only spirits robed in different masks, for the enemy has always been after the identity of the church. Why is this? Because our identity is linked and connected to the destiny God has in store for us. Before you can walk and be effective in your destiny, before you can be a powerful minister of God in what He has called you to do, you must become *one* with your identity and radically embrace your Apostolic identity. This is the foundation of your entire life and calling. Some of us are too concerned with what we are supposed to do for the Kingdom when we need to quit worrying about what we are supposed to be doing and embrace who we are supposed to be. When you become one with your Apostolic identity, all the promises God has made to you will flow from that foundation.

Recently, at a Christian Life College summit, my husband, Pastor Nathaniel Haney, spoke to the entire faculty and staff about the importance of protecting, guarding, and embracing our Apostolic identity in a career- and education-driven world. We are not against education, especially as an educational facility, but there is a place where education and philosophy can come to the place they overrule and overpower our identity as Apostolic people. I want to share the powerful Word that was brought to us that day by our pastor:

> Daniel, at thirteen years old, went into three to four years of intense training that was sixteen hours a day. He learned the Chaldean tongue, Aramaic; and of course, he knew Hebrew. When you read the Book of Daniel, you realize he was being taught witchcraft, the occult. They were taught to read the stars and how to read the livers of goats to gain understanding. These students were taught how to communicate with the dead and all kinds

of occult practices, and for three years, a thirteen-year-old boy was forced to sit under godless and mystic instructors. But the Bible says this about young Daniel:

> But Daniel purposed in his heart that he would not defile himself with the portion of the king's meat. (Daniel 1:8)

What made Daniel different? He understood his education was to be used as a tool but was not intended to become his identity. Education has a way of making people lean to their own understanding; it can make people become arrogant and think more highly of themselves than they ought.

One of the most arrogant spirits in the world is in the universities in America, and God's people must be aware of this. One of the most rebellious and lawless spirits in the world is going to be in the universities. The Scripture states that "pride goeth before destruction" and that "God resisteth the proud," and He has not changed and He will not change. I want to tell someone reading this today that you do not have to lose your identity to an educational institution!

Moses had to sit for thirty years with Egyptian tutors who did not believe in the God of his mother and father. Even though he was under the instruction of the greatest tutors and the smartest of intellectual minds of his day, he never sold out his God or his identity. The Bible says when he *came to age* he went to visit his people. Moses never forgot who his people were even when he had to sit through all levels of education, learn their many languages, and become skilled in the business of

Egypt as he was being groomed for a court position
or maybe even the place of Pharaoh. A thousand
others crumbled under and said, "I'll give the devil
my best, and I'll use it for my short-lived life here
on this earth."

These men of faith were smarter than most of
us, men who had more education than most of us,
men who were forced into learning almost to the
point of losing their lives. These men were some
of the greatest men that the Bible writes about,
but what made them great? Was it their education? No. The Bible doesn't talk too much about
their intense education, but there is much written
regarding their relationship with God. We read
about these men seeking the face of God, setting
aside seasons of extended fasting, seeing visions,
and having God speak to them through dreams,
revealing the future. These are the things that made
them great and effective and remembered as heroes
of the faith.

Daniel got into prayer one day by the riverbank.
As he entered into praying and fasting, the entire
realm of the spirit of two nations collided. When is
the last time you prayed so intensely that the angels
had to start moving and the devils couldn't sit still?
These were men used powerfully by God who had
levels of education but *never let education become who
they were*. If God's ministers get to the place they
are so academically minded or so concerned about
money, so concerned about getting an overload
of information into the brain, they will lose their
identity, and the kingdom of God will suffer greatly.
If that be so, God will raise up another group of
people who will become consumed with a love for
Apostolic identity in our place.

We are an Apostolic people from the conception of the church. We live by the doctrines of the first-century church. We are not just a group of people, but we are Apostolic! We are the people who are called to walk in the Spirit and will continue to bring the identity of the true church to this world. I don't want a spiritual plastic surgeon getting hold of the church and making it look nice on the outside so the world will accept it. It doesn't matter if the world accepts us; we may be *in* this world but we are not of this world! We are here to please the head, Jesus Christ our King, and that is all that matters at the end of the day.

Some of the most miserable people in the world are those who have never learned how to embrace and love their Apostolic identity. When we do not realize who we are supposed to be and who God has called us to be, we begin to let go of little things, thinking they are not that important. There is a reason why I dress the way I dress, there is a reason why I act like I act, sing like I sing, worship like I worship. This is the DNA that came from my mother, which is the church, and from my father, who is God Almighty.

Through the years, I have watched solid young adults, who have graduated with their bachelor's degrees from Pentecostal Bible colleges, jump into seminary studies. Without having a shepherd to guide them when they had questions, they ended up in spiritual disaster. Link up with someone who has spiritual authority in your life, ask him or her to walk with you through the educational process, and *go to that person* when your doctrines are being questioned or attacked. Trust me, it will happen! The god of this world would love for the ministers of the Lord to get entangled with the religious world's philosophies and stir them into the mixing pot of doctrinal confusion.

Claudette Walker comments on the importance of having a voice in your life:

> I believe it is so important for us to let God lead us to godly mentors who are older than us. We can glean so much from them. We all need someone in our lives who can tell us when we are wrong. We also need the encouragement those people can give us from their years of experience. At my age of sixty-six, I love giving an encouraging word to younger ladies in ministry, and often all it takes is a listening ear. I have made so many mistakes in my life. I love to go ahead of them and warn them of a pitfall ahead I fell into once; I love telling them about a stone in the path ahead they need to be careful not to trip over. However, we need to be careful not to make the mentor take the place of Jesus to us. There is a danger of leaning too much and too often on another person. Balance is the key to all of life. I thank God for the women who have walked alongside me and listened with their ears and hearts when I have been confused or troubled or overwhelmed. I have gleaned so very much from them. Now I want to repay the debt I owe by offering my ears to listen, my heart to care, my spirit to pray, and when directed by God, His words to counsel as needed.

If one will look at the history of the church, she will see that Satan has been most effective in derailing the church through mixing into the teachings of the church the philosophies of man. This produces a perversion of the truth, which eventually becomes heresy. The enemy will do anything he can to get this powerful doctrine watered down. This is not a new problem because the apostle Paul fought this same spirit that tried to creep into the church:

> As ye have therefore received Christ Jesus the Lord, so walk ye in him: rooted and built up in him, and stablished in the faith, as ye have been taught, abounding therein with thanksgiving. Beware lest any man spoil you through philosophy and vain deceit, after the tradition of men, after the rudiments of the world, and not after Christ. (Colossians 2:6–8)

Paul was trying to explain to God-called men and women that the work of God is not a matter of eloquent and educated talk but a Spirit-empowered walk that is Spirit-led!

Matthew Henry Commentary says this:

> There is a philosophy, which rightly exercises our reasonable faculties; a study of the works of God, which leads us to the knowledge of God, and confirms our faith in him. But there is a philosophy, which is vain and deceitful; and while it pleases men's fancies, hinders their faith: such are curious speculations about things above us, or no concern to us.

Barnes Commentary says this:

> Beware lest any man spoil you—the word "spoil" now commonly means, to corrupt, to cause to decay

and perish, as fruit is spoiled by keeping too long, or paper by wetting, or hay by a long rain, or crops by mildew. But the Greek word used here means to spoil in the sense of plunder, rob, as when plunder is taken in war. The meaning is, "Take heed lest anyone plunder or rob you of your faith and hope by philosophy." These false teachers would strip them of their faith and hope, as an invading army would rob a country of all that was valuable.

Now, before you get offended at my last statement, let me clarify. I am not against Christian psychology *in its place*. I have a dear and close friend who has been a Christian psychologist for years. She has helped hundreds of people through the years work through some tough situations, and I personally have recommended certain people to her. But here is the difference: she is a woman of faith, she is a woman who prays and walks with God, and this is the career path she has chosen. She has learned how to set boundaries when it comes to the philosophy of the world mixing with what the Word declares, and she knows the difference and is not afraid or intimidated to call the dividing line. She is a student of the Word, which gives her the right perspective when responding to situations. She is also under the authority of her husband and her pastor, which, in turn, gives her spiritual authority over evil spirits that are opposing these people she is counseling.

A call of God is of the highest order, and those who feel this supernatural calling must be careful not to dilute or allow what Paul called the "rudiments of this world" and "philosophy and vain deceit" to get mixed in with this divine summons. Satan, through the centuries, has tried to infiltrate his methods into the brain of the ministry because he knows this: what the ministers feed on will be what they feed God's sheep.

Paul was not against education, but he warned his readers to be aware of the enemy's tactics and he did this by exposing them. He exposed an age-old method of attack against the church and the ministry as he uncovered anything under the "mask" of Christianity that elevates academic ideas about God above what the Word of God declares or over our spiritual relationship and commitment.

I don't know about you, but when I go to a church event or conference to hear a certain teacher or speaker and I have been facing great difficulty in my life or am in great need of a word from God, I want to know that the man or woman of God who is speaking into my life is a person who walks in the Spirit. I want to know that minister prays and seeks after the Lord and is someone who holds fast to the teachings of the Bible— not just what he or she has learned in seminary or from a book. This generation so desperately needs women who are Spirit-led and have kept their feet to the old paths. You think about the women who have affected you the most in your walk with God, and I guarantee they were people who knew how to pray and lived a life of consecration and sacrifice. They were women who walked in the Spirit.

There is no substitution for the old paths There is no other way to walk under the anointing of God!

GUARDING YOUR HEART

I grew up in Oklahoma in the home of men who love to hunt, and when fall rolled around, the deer saw more of them than their family did. It was not uncommon to come home to a dinner table filled with wild game of all sorts, some more alluring than others. Even though I'm not a hunter myself, being raised in that atmosphere I learned a lot (whether I liked it or not) about how to kill prey. One thing I learned is the hunter has an agenda. He doesn't come just to take a stroll through the forest or enjoy the weather, he is not interested in bird watching or rock climbing, but he has a purpose to his visit. And this results in another steak on the dinner table.

When a hunter zeroes in on his prey, the crosshairs of his scope are centered on a vital location: the heart. If the heart of that animal can become damaged or wounded, it will die, and it's the same with us. Your enemy knows that your heart is what rules your life, and in turn, it determines your destination. The condition of our heart affects every area of our lives, and *in this place* the enemy of our soul will first attack us.

If he can get us to give in to the damaging emotions of bitterness, jealousy, envy, or pride, his attacks will prove fatal as the bullet of offense makes its way into the heart of a woman of God. David, who undoubtedly had to fight these bitter emotions during the attacks that came through Saul, wrote these words:

> For, lo, the wicked bend their bow, they make ready their arrow upon the string, that they may privily [or secretly] shoot at the upright in heart. If

the foundations be destroyed, what can the righteous do? (Psalm 11:2–3)

The enemy knows if our hearts become cracked or damaged in the slightest way, it will affect every area of our life and ministry. We cannot control the offenses or hurts that come to us, but we can control how we respond to them. Secrecy is the greatest weapon the enemy will use to keep his arrows festering and poisoning our hearts, and as long as we keep them secret, release and healing can never come.

R. T. Kendall, who was the pastor of Westminster Chapel in London for twenty-five years, shares his experience of how bitterness tried to destroy him:

> Most of us have times in our lives when we are pushed to our limits as to how much we are called to forgive. I remember what happened to me with such clarity. I have vowed not to retell this story, but suffice it to say I had never been hurt so deeply, before or since. The wrong I believe was done to me affected just about every area of my life; my family, my ministry, my very sense of self-worth. Nobody should have to tell a mature minister of the gospel of Christ the most obvious and fundamental teaching of the New Testament. But there I was in the ministry of our Lord Jesus Christ, filled with so much hurt and bitterness that I could hardly fulfill my duties.
>
> I had only told Josif [who was a friend of his] of my problem because I thought I would get sympathy from a man I deeply respected and who I thought would be on my side. I expected him to put his arm on my shoulder and say, "R. T., you are right to feel so angry! Tell me all about it.

Get it out of your system." Because Josif was from Romania and was far removed from the situation, I was able to tell him everything.

"Is that all?" he asked when I finished my story.

"Yes, that's it," I said.

And then came those remarkable words—spoken in his Romanian accent: "You must totally forgive them."

"I can't," I replied.

"You can, and you must," he insisted. Unsatisfied with his response, I tried to continue. "R. T.," he interrupted, "you must totally forgive them. Release them, and you will be set free."[7]

I had to make an important decision: Which do I prefer—the peace or the bitterness? I couldn't have it both ways. I began to see that I was the one who was losing by nursing my attitude of unforgiveness. My bitterness wasn't damaging anyone but myself. I have come to believe that the only way to move beyond the hurt and go forward in life is through total forgiveness.

Jesus warned us that offenses will come, and Peter said not to be shocked when fiery trials come to test you. Just remember every attack and every trial will be centered on damaging the territory of your heart. It would be a great success for Satan to be able to hang the heads of women of God upon the hallways of Hell as a trophy display. It's not a question if bitterness, jealousy, pride, envy will ever come knocking at your door; it's a promise. But when it does, you must recognize what the attack is aimed at!

I don't know why this seems to be a pattern in my life, but many times when God is desiring to take me to a new level of the Spirit or He desires to use me in a special way that accompanies a new anointing, I will go through a season of crushing first. Brokenness, hurt, offense, bitterness—they have all been used at various times to bring about a humbling and crushing in my spirit as the hand of the Potter sees things inside me that must come out before I can be used. Paul talked about "dying daily," and Jesus Himself "became obedient unto death." There is pain involved in death. It hurts to die. There is a crushing of our flesh, belittling of our image. Pain and hurt are always involved with dying.

A few months ago, I was in the car with my girls, coming home from an event. I ran into someone at this event, whom I had been struggling with inside my heart for a while, over a situation in which *I had every right to justify* my feelings toward this one. What the person had done was unethical and wrong. I had prayed about it several times and released it to God, but I knew those feelings were still alive. You know those times when you want to *grab your purse and run out the back door* when you see that person. But since this person was "out of sight out of mind," I just kept pushing my feelings back down into my spirit.

Driving home that day, in conversation with my four girls, I began to make some negative remarks about this individual, and I noticed the car became very quiet. All of a sudden, from the back seat, my youngest daughter, who was thirteen at the time, blurted out, "Mom, you need to quit saying negative things about that person. You have gotten bitter over that person."

Talk about trying to swallow a tree trunk while you're driving! I was speechless. I was embarrassed. I could feel the hair on my arms beginning to stand up and red crawling up my neck, and my first reaction was: "Hey, I'm the mom and I will defend my position," But I *knew* what was spoken out of the mouth of my thirteen-year-old girl was the truth, and I was embarrassed to admit it.

I carried that heaviness all day long until the next day. I knew I had to confront this spirit head-on, for I have encountered bitterness before and knew how damaging it could be. That next morning I made my way into the empty sanctuary, and all alone with God, I repented, cried, and dug out all the rocks of bitterness that had been exposed the day before. But this time, I told God I would make it right.

You know why? I don't want my vessel to end up in the Potter's field! I've come too far in this thing, I've dealt with too many issues, I've wrestled too many devils, I've fought too many battles, and I've lived for God too many years to let bitterness bring me down!

I don't care how uncomfortable it is, how embarrassing, how humiliating, how crushing to my flesh, or belittling to my image. I want the hand of the Potter to have access to my vessel in every season of my life.

Sometimes you have to take physical actions in order to destroy that root of bitterness totally and allow healing to flow, and I knew this is what God was requiring of me. The next day I made a phone call. I cried and humbled myself before this person and asked for forgiveness; I made things right. When I did, the heaviness that only bitterness can bring lifted off me in an instant, and I felt the presence of God come upon me in a powerful way. Something I had been reaching for in the Spirit was imparted to me the instant I obeyed God, and I will never forget the anointing that rested upon me when I spoke at a conference the next week. I feel in the Holy Ghost right now that God is speaking directly to someone reading this, and your breakthrough, your next level of anointing will come only when you're willing to take the steps to destroy the root of bitterness. You cannot move forward until you remove and confront the obstacles that hinder the Spirit from moving in your life.

I'm not going to join the vessels in the Potter's field because I refused to deal with bitterness! I'm not going to join those forsaken vessels just because I was treated wrong or someone offended me! I trust the hand of the Potter, and whatever He says to do to get rid of it, I trust Him enough to step out and do it. It takes faith to forgive someone who has hurt you, faith in God that when you obey Him and do things His way, He will step in on your behalf and fight the things you are not able to fight!

Friend, an anointing and power will be able to flow in your life when your vessel is kept clean. The pure Spirit of God cannot flow through a pipe that is laden with rust, for the rust will cause impurities to flow. The Spirit can flow freely and powerfully through a vessel that is not perfect but is willing constantly to confront, destroy, and uproot the residue of attacks that center upon our hearts.

Rejoice not against me, O mine enemy: when I fall, I shall arise; when I sit in darkness, the LORD shall be a light unto me. (Micah 7:8)

Go forth in the name of Jesus and in the spirit of obedience and He will fight the battles you cannot fight.

7 | *Pursuing the Call*

Working with many precious college students who feel a call of God upon their lives, I have watched through the years how the painful process of waiting on God's direction and timing has brought out the best and worst in people. These students spend up to four years working hard, studying, consecrating, dedicating to the call of God with the assumption that as soon as graduation hits, the doors of ministry will fly wide open for them. Many times, or I should say rather, most of the time that is not the case. There is a process of growth that requires a raw, sheer faith in knowing God still sees you even in your time of waiting. We will always have times of struggles and times of testing, and every season will bring different types of tests. The Lord has a purpose in not allowing us to be fruitful and advancing all the time, knowing we need seasons of struggle. As hard as they may be to go through, the times we struggle remind us of our extreme dependence upon God and choke out the pride of our own ability.

You see, God is not so much interested in building a ministry as He is in building the minister. God doesn't view ministry like we view ministry. He puts all His efforts into building the heart and the foundation of that minister, the soul and character of that minister, and He escorts us to a seat in His waiting room to accomplish this task. God's waiting room is so important and so transforming that if you were able to skip this process, something vital would be forever missing in the foundation of your calling. But this place is sometimes so unpleasant we are blinded to this fact. Some things are God's will, but they are not God's timing. If we do not realize this, we lose our faith in God and forfeit our ministry all because we don't understand there must be times of development.

God takes His time to develop us and mold us into something He can use and depend upon, and the development always happens in a lonely place on the backside of a desert. Moses was God's chosen man to lead the people of Israel, and even with the supernatural experiences he had confirming his calling, he still had to wait for thirty years until the doors began to open. I'm sure he hated every minute of it, but he never lost who he was. Can you imagine how Moses felt, once a prince in the courts of Pharaoh's house, skilled and trained with the highest of degrees, now on the backside of the desert shoveling sheep manure? God was shaping him through loneliness and a seemingly deserted call of God, surrounded by sheep, flies, and barren hillsides.

My dear friend, don't try to bypass the season where your foundation is being built. Just because God has spoken to you and called you to some form or area of ministry or just because He anoints you to function in a particular area doesn't mean your foundation is built and you have arrived. Think about David. God had Samuel anoint David as king over Israel, but immediately he was sent back into the fields to feed and take care of the smelly sheep. Don't get discouraged while you're on hold, get *a hold of God* during this time and develop your relationship with Him. Allow Him to develop the minister, not the ministry.

You're not in a race with others, and you don't have to prove anything to anyone else. You're on God's time clock, and when you understand this, a certain peace comes even when you're on hold and everybody else has a green light. Great growth does not come through mountaintop experiences; great growth comes through valleys, ditches, and times in your life when you feel vulnerable, empty, and spent. God will move in His greatest ways during the lowest times of your life—not during times of blessing and increase. Blessings are appreciated and recognized only once you have gone through times of silence and loneliness and all your dreams have been seemingly aborted.

Claudette Walker talks about waiting on God:

My husband and I had been married for nine years, and I had done all I knew to be by my husband's side. Since he had a passion for quizzing, I began to keep score even though I had never seen a buzzer before. This led to a national ministry, where we were blessed to minister to thousands of brilliant and dedicated youth. I am not a good musician, but since he led the choir, I tried to play the organ and piano.

When we worked beside Pastor J. T. Pugh in Odessa, Texas, my husband felt to start a carpenter's shop to reach unsaved youth, so I helped deliver Alpo dog food to raise money to redecorate the building.

Even though the Lord had called me to teach His Word seventeen years before, I had assumed it mostly had to do with helping my husband however I could. And that was true. God may call you to some area of ministry, but you will usually have years to prove that calling by serving another. David was called of God and anointed to be king, but for years he simply cared for sheep on the hillside and then for years after that ran from murderous Saul.

I will never forget the first time I felt the powerful anointing of the Lord. Mary Alice Paslay was an ordained minister, and she had preached powerful revival meetings as a young girl. She was my pastor's wife, and I loved her so, for she was my spiritual mother in the faith. We had been invited to speak together at the West Virginia ladies' retreat. I was thirty-two years old at the time, and God had called me seventeen years prior to teach His Word. I had faithfully taught Sunday school and ministered to youth, but I had never experienced the anointing as I did that day. We had both been asked to be on a panel. I felt intimidated to answer because I was a kid compared to Sister Paslay. However, one question was asked of me during the panel, so I dutifully opened my mouth. A well of powerful anointing oil began to gush from my innermost being. I knew things to say I did not even know I knew. My spirit had tapped into some source and fire that was ignited in my spirit. I can still recall the wonder of that fire as I looked at others to see if they felt it too.

In one instant I knew what the Lord would do through me in the future. I knew He would open doors. I knew that I would *never try to force a door open*. I knew that when I got to the pulpit He would provide, that God would also give me His words for the people, and that His anointing would flow through me. How could a very young lady know all that in one instant? It was because for seventeen years I had submitted myself to God, to my husband's authority, and to my pastor. No one's journey is the same, but I have rarely talked to someone whose pattern did not fit the general plan of God. First comes *a genuine call from the Lord,* a time and season of *testing and faithfulness,* a fresh anointing, then doors *opened by the Lord* for the ministry He gave you.

God spoke to Joseph through vivid dreams that he would be exalted and used mightily as the hand of God was upon his life. God began to unfold to him his future and where that direction would take him, but Joseph was young. Maybe through sheer excitement he began to announce to his brothers the dreams and visions God had given to him. But because of his lack of wisdom and spiritual immaturity, what seemed to him as a positive move was indeed a negative move. When he began to announce and proclaim to those around him that God was going to use him in this way or in this area, he began to release to the outside world the visions and dreams God had given to him. Thus, he caused great jealousy to arise in his brethren, which eventually turned to hatred and disgust.

Maybe God has shown you a specific area or calling that He desires to bring you to, but learn a hard lesson from Joseph and read between the lines regarding the announcement of your ministry or in what ways God is using you. Who knows whether Joseph's life would have taken another turn, or if he would have saved himself from much grief and pain if he had learned as a young man to ponder in his heart the things God had shown him.

Donna Linville talks about how to respond to God and to your calling while on hold:

> The first thing I would say would be to establish an altar of *seek ye first the kingdom*. This is important because we can be selective of what we want to pursue. We may have in our minds a vision of great, grandiose things involving a powerful ministry. I found at the very beginning of my ministry God wanted me to build an altar of "seeking Him first," so I had to accept the most mundane, the most humbling ministries. I stepped forth and accepted anything in the kingdom of God that was asked of me; it was a test to see if I was willing, whether it was teaching Sunday school, going on outreach, or playing an accordion during a jailhouse ministry. Because I had this feeling that God was asking me to seek Him first or seek His kingdom first, I had to have first a *desire* for His kingdom, so I applied myself to every facet that came to me. I had to first seek His kingdom, in whatever dimension or area that was, to initiate me into the kingdom of the ministry. We can sit back and wait for the image of what we think our ministry ought to be instead of seeking whatever door is opening for us at that time.

I believe that because I said yes to everything, the desire to be used by God was being developed inside me. Every time I did puppets or taught little five-year-olds, it seemed as if God began to grow and something began to burn in my spirit. Not only is it a test, but it's a growing of the spirit of usage. When God started growing that inside me, through being involved in any area of ministry that opened for me through those years (choir, jail ministry, etc.), I think somehow the altar was burning brighter and brighter until all that consumed me was a desire to work for Jesus and to be used by God. Eventually, the Lord was the One who presented the opportunities due to the fact I started saying yes to whatever He presented to me at the first altar. The first altar was teaching five-year-olds with puppets, and before that I was cleaning the church. I felt that whatever was asked was an opportunity to prove to God that I was seeking His kingdom first, and when God acknowledged I was seeking His kingdom, He opened His kingdom to me. It all started with the little things.

I believe the concept of "pulpit ministry" can keep you sitting on the pew the rest of your life. God does not promote what He doesn't allow to sit on the wheel of the Potter first. I do not believe the ministry is always behind the pulpit or even speaking in front of people, but I do believe if that is in God's plan for you, you will be acclimated to that place little by little.

Many times, a young lady feels she cannot be used or put to use in God's kingdom until she's married, and everything mentally is put on hold until that happens. Singleness is something that can be a great blessing and gift in your life. Being single is not something you need to be "cured" of, as it is not a disease. Being single is not a curse or a plague. When you are single, you are still a whole person. If you don't understand this concept, you will begin to think you're just a fraction of a person or half a person who will never be complete until that someone comes along and *completes* you.

If the right young man does come along, he should be joining with a whole person—a young lady who already is involved in some area of ministry and has found purpose in her life while she is single. Debbie Saiz, who is my friend and now a pastor's wife in Long Beach, California, was raised in a pastor's home and felt a call to ministry at a young age. Debbie was single for many years and did not get married until she was in her forties. But instead of waiting around and looking for someone to fulfill her, she put her hand to the plow and allowed God to use her and fulfill that call upon her life while she was single.

I have asked Debbie Saiz to share her story:

> None of us like to wait, yet in life we have to wait on so many things. I live in Los Angeles, and I wait in traffic. We wait in the security line at the airport. We wait in line on a plane on the tarmac for takeoff. We wait in line for Black Friday sales. We wait for the doctor. Waiting on the Lord to open doors may be one of the most difficult aspects of the Christian life. So what do we do in the meantime? What do we do while we wait?
>
> Waiting is God's way of seeing if we will trust Him before we move forward. In the waiting, we are reminded that God is in control and that we are

not in charge. Waiting allows God to do His work in His time. We must remember that His timing is best and what God *does in us* while we wait is as important as what we are waiting for. But waiting does not mean doing nothing. Waiting is the confident, expectant, active, disciplined, and sometimes painful clinging to God.

When I was around the age of thirteen, my dad preached a sermon about the book, *Jonathan Livingston Seagull*. Jonathan was a seagull who realized that he was not like the other seagulls. He was told, "The difference between you and the other seagulls is that you have begun to understand who you really are and have begun to practice it." As a young girl, I had a dream that someday I would be used of God. I was not exactly sure what that entailed, but I knew I was different and that I had a call upon my life. Even at a young age, I, like Jonathan, began to understand who I was and began to follow after my call and practice it through being involved in different ministries.

In my twenties, I realized that I was not like most girls. I didn't get married right away like many of my friends even though I had the desire to and always knew that I would meet the right guy. Marriage didn't come when I thought it would. I realized that God had a specific plan for my life, and in order for it to come to pass, I had to let Him unfold His plan. Giving God complete control of your heart and life is a lot easier said than done! I learned early on that God gives the best to those who leave the choice to Him.

While in university, I wrote a paper about *carpe diem*, "seize the day." I realized that I had to make the best of *now*. I had to bloom where I was planted and live the apostle Paul's words of learning to be content in whatever state I was in. Someone said, "Don't cry over the past; it's gone. Don't stress about the future; it has yet to arrive. Live in the present and make it beautiful!" My mom always told me that one's calling will open doors, and I began to realize that I didn't have to try to open doors for things to happen. If I would seek God and live a dedicated life to Him, He would open the right doors at the right time. I was seated in a front-row seat with my seatbelt buckled when God blew my mind with the doors that He was opening to me as a young woman.

I remember the Sunday night in my early twenties; I was standing in the altar area praying with some young people in our church when I heard an audible voice speak to me, "This is where I want you." I turned around to see who was talking to me. The people around me all had their eyes shut and were praying. I heard it again. I turned around again to see if someone was there. When I heard it a third time, I knew it was God speaking to me. I was in total awe that He would speak to me that way.

Now I had direction that God wanted me to work with youth. I was not sure exactly what or where, but I knew I needed to take a step. I talked to my pastor, and he had me talk to our Sunday school coordinator. They put me in the high-school juniors and seniors Sunday school class, and two weeks later, both teachers' husbands got job transfers and I found myself the main teacher. I began to research about teaching youth and found some teaching helps that opened up a whole new way of ministry for me. I was not the best teacher, but I gave it my best. I found that the old saying, "Students don't care how much you know until they know how much you care," was true. I was pouring myself into these students throughout the week as well as Sundays.

A couple years later, our youth pastor moved and my dad (who was also my pastor) talked to me about taking this position. I remember sitting in his office thinking that a youth pastor was a man's job. I didn't know a woman who was a full-time youth pastor, and I wondered if a woman could do it. My dad reminded me of all the exciting things that were happening with the juniors and seniors in my Sunday school class, and he asked me to pray about it. I did, and the more I prayed the more I knew it was God calling me. I stepped into the unknown, walking where Joshua 3:4 talks about, "For you have not passed this way heretofore." I knew I had to walk where God was leading me. When I stepped out in faith, He gave me a deep love and burden for youth ministry.

It seldom occurred to me that I was a woman in a man's world of ministry. I was the only girl born into a home with three older brothers, so God had prepared me for this role all my life. I faced a lot of obstacles as a woman in a man's world of ministry in those days, but when you know that you are called of God to do what you are doing, you keep trudging on, following your call. I'm thankful for the great support that I had, for I was also raised in a home with parents and brothers who encouraged me. My pastor and church supported me as well as my district superintendent; it was important that all areas of authority accepted my ministry.

My dad taught me something very powerful when he said these words, "Men recognize women's abilities as well as their submission." As a woman in ministry, I have always been submitted to men in leadership. I was blessed to be raised in a district with some amazing women who were involved in ministry like Vesta Mangun, Thetus Tenney, and Joan Ewing. All three were used greatly in ministry and they all had great influence in my life in the state of Louisiana.

After fourteen years as a youth pastor, I felt God leading me to step out and travel full time. I had been blessed to travel occasionally, but to step out and go full time was a whole new level of trust for me. I did not know women in our ranks who were doing that at the time, and it was a scary thing to leave the comforts of my full-time job as a youth pastor and to step into the unknown. No one knew outside my immediate family of what I was feeling and praying about, but when God calls, He will confirm that call. I received different confirmations from people who knew nothing. A visiting preacher on a Wednesday night, just before he preached, went to the keyboard and said, "Debbie, I wrote this song and just feel that tonight I'm supposed to sing it to you." He started singing the words, "You're going in the right direction."

A few weeks later, I spoke at our Louisiana ladies' conference, and after the service, Joan Ewing came to me and told me that while I was speaking she had a quick vision of me traveling all over from church to church. She said that she was not sure what it meant, but she knew God wanted her to tell me. These were confirmations to me that I was moving in the direction God was leading me, and as scary as it was, I stepped into full-time traveling ministry. I was *not* a licensed minister but was amazed, as I took this step, how doors began to open. I was in Virginia speaking at their youth camp when I received a call from Pastor Kenneth Haney in Stockton, California, and that one phone call led to many times of ministry at Christian Life Center in Stockton, which led to many other doors of ministry opening for me across the country.

My mom always told me that my knight in shining armor would come one day, riding in for me. I believed that. I felt that God had the right one for me and that I was not going to settle for any less than what God had for me. I decided to wait on God, pursuing all He had for me while I was single. I knew I had a promise from God that the right one was coming, and I had to wait. Waiting on God is not easy, but it does increase your strength. It goes against the grain of our quick-fix microwave mentality of thinking, and we have to be reminded from time to time that good things come to those who wait. I have seen too many young ladies who want to get married and settle for a substitute rather than waiting for God's promise. I made up my mind that would not be me, but I would wait. In the waiting, I continued to follow God's leading, and as I delighted myself in Him, He would give me the desires of my heart

I had been traveling for almost two years when I received a call late one Saturday night at my hotel. It was Pastor Larson telling me that his mother had fallen and broken her hip, and he asked if I would speak the next morning to the church. I had been taught that when God opens a door, you don't question it; you just walk through it. I told him that I would. After I got off the phone, it hit me that even though I had spoken across the country, I had not spoken to a Sunday morning congregation. I immediately called my dad and mom, and they encouraged me that I could do this.

I was up most of the night praying and studying, and I remember standing on the platform that morning at Revival Tabernacle with several ministers (who were all men) thinking, *God, I'm a woman. What am I doing here?* I will never forget the message I spoke that morning, and as I spoke, I felt the anointing of the Holy Ghost and knew I was speaking what God wanted. I flew home for Thanksgiving a couple days later, and as I was landing, I felt a stirring in my heart that change in my life was coming. I was unsure what this meant and what all God had for me in my future. I just knew change was coming.

That January, I went with my sister-in-law, Gayla, to Landmark Conference in Stockton where she was speaking. I remember standing in the altar and felt God leading me to go home and build an altar. That next week, I was back home in Louisiana and felt to go on a three-day fast. My parents were out of town, so I had the ranch to myself. I remember lying on the floor in the great room praying and seeking God, telling Him that I knew I was called to ministry and that I wanted ministry for my future as I gave myself once again to God. Giving yourself is not a one-time thing but must be repeated at various seasons in one's life.

A few weeks later, on a Sunday night after speaking at a church in Virginia, the pastor told me that he felt led to pray for me. He and his wife laid hands upon me, and I felt the Holy Ghost so strong that all I could do was raise my hands like a funnel as I felt something fresh flowing into me. Sitting in the pastor's office after the service, he told me that he felt like a fresh and new anointing was flowing into me. I was not sure what all God was doing, but I was excited and ready to see! I did not give thought to the fact that when a fresh anointing comes, there usually is a breaking that brings the fresh anointing. I wanted to be used deeper in God. I felt changed after I had built that altar and prayed for God to use me.

You can become bitter or better through situations that come your way in life. I realized that God was reaching for me through my hurt and pain, and He was calling me to go deeper. In the midst of my brokenness, I turned to deeper prayer, seeking God and studying His Word. I remember on a Sunday afternoon at my brother and sister-in-law's home in Dallas, I went into the study next to the guest room where I was staying, and I had a great prayer meeting. I dispatched angels and really felt that I gave some things to God. God was working on me, telling me to quit worrying and trust Him. The office was dimly lit, and I felt drawn to a book. It was Lloyd John Ogilvie's book, *Praying with Power*. As I opened it, this paragraph jumped out at me:

> The cure of worry is not just the belief that things will work out for good under the providence of God. It comes from wrenching our egos from the throne of our hearts. Worry is a manifestation that we are still living with our wills in control and our desires as the focus of our prayers. The worry syndrome is seldom broken until we are willing to be called into prayer to receive God's orders for what is best rather than tenaciously grasping what we are determined to convince him should be done.

In the season of waiting, as the years go by, you have to realize that in these times of pouring your heart out to the Lord, He does some of His greatest work in you. In those times when we feel like we are in the desert or in the wilderness, God brings hope, gives us visions and dreams, and works deep things in our heart. These times of waiting allow us to know God more intimately, and our relationship with Him grows deeper. We just have to trust God and quit watching the time clock of our life, thinking that the world is passing us by.

Many times when my mom was sharing and speaking to ladies, she would say, "Ladies are to look like a girl, act like a lady, think like a man, and work like a dog!" So very true!

After one of my first dates with my soon-to-be husband, a pastor friend of his told him that I would be one of the few women he would allow in his pulpit because I acted like a lady, embraced being feminine, and didn't try to act like a man. That meant a lot to my husband. Young lady, men want ladies to be ladies! It is a big turnoff to many men to see a woman in any ministry who does not act like a lady. You can be a lady and still be called of God in any type of ministry.

You never know what God has in store for you as you go along living life, doing what He has called you to do. That day in Alexandria, Louisiana, I sat next to a preacher from southern California who had a single preacher friend, and it occurred to him that he needed to introduce us. God orders our steps and is working when we can't see it or have any idea of what is going on. You can't just sit around waiting for the right man to come along in your life; I never had that attitude or feeling. I always knew that I had a promise and that the right one would come at the right time, but to be honest I didn't know that I was going to have to wait so long. But the wait was well worth it. Every path that God led me on throughout my life has led me to where I am today.

Nothing that has happened to you is a surprise to God—He will get you to where you are supposed to be. You may be waiting on your promise, seeking direction from God for your life, or whatever you are waiting on, but don't lose hope. Keep seeking Him with your whole heart, following His leading. He is preparing you for tremendous growth and working in ways that you can't see. In times of waiting, my soul is revived and my spirit is renewed. Isaiah wrote:

> But those who trust in the LORD will find new strength. They will soar high on wings like eagles. They will run and not grow weary. They will walk and not faint." (Isaiah 40:31, NLT)

Take the limits off God. Not only will He meet your needs, but He will give you the desires of your heart. God's best is worth fighting and praying for and well worth waiting for. As I have said already, God does give the best to those who leave the choice to Him.

God does everything by appointment. He has a predestined, appointed time for your doors of ministry to begin to open, and in spite of temporary circumstances and void, lonely silences, He still has His hand upon your life. I just feel that someone reading this right now needed to hear that. The enemy cannot hinder or abort the plan of God for our lives, but he can attack our faith and get us to the place of discouragement where we think God has forgotten us. When we understand God works through seasons and even in our lonely, barren seasons, He is working in us.

> To every thing there is a season, and a time to every purpose under the heaven. (Ecclesiastes 3:1)

> And he changeth the times and the seasons: he removeth kings, and setteth up kings: he giveth wisdom unto the wise, and knowledge to them that know understanding. (Daniel 2:21)

> And let us not be weary in well doing: for in due season we shall reap, if we faint not. (Galatians 6:9)

God has a plan, and we can either understand why we are going through lonely times of waiting and accept God's timetable or be crushed by it through self-pity or impatience. Whatever place you find yourself in right now, do your work with all your might, for you just may be in a season of testing. Reap the fruit from the season you're in right now instead of looking at it through a distorted lens; prove to God that whatever state you are in, you will be content in His will.

Elsy Cunningham makes this statement regarding seasons:

> Pulpit ministry is not the only ministry in the church. Find your niche where God wants you to minister, and flourish there! In our church, we have a new worshiper's team, and I have an integral role in this ministry. As a home missionary's wife, I developed a personal ministry and calling to assimilate people into the church. This has evolved

into a productive ministry in retaining people in the church as I personally find ways to connect new worshipers with seasoned saints of God. Because I am closely connected to the families in our church, God has given me an ability to know where and when to integrate new members. Many of our saints credit this ministry and the Lord for keeping them in the church, and it's all because I have learned how to be fulfilled in whatever door is opened for me in that season of my life.

About eighteen years ago, my son was just born and we had moved into a new neighborhood where I did not know anyone. I remember sitting on the pew during a Wednesday night Bible study, when out of nowhere the Lord spoke into my spirit, "Start a neighborhood ladies' Bible study in your new neighborhood." Well, here I was a young mother with a new baby and two other little kids at home. I did not know how I was going to fit that into my schedule, but the tug on my spirit would not quit. For days and into weeks those same words would come to me over and over again, "Start a ladies' Bible study in your neighborhood." I knew God was speaking to me, but nobody else knew it. I could have easily made excuses as to why I wasn't able to do this right now, and no one would have known except God and me. But this was a testing time for me, to see if I would be sensitive to the Lord's voice and be willing to step out in faith.

The Lord brought to my attention how Jesus always commissioned His disciples to go out in pairs, and I thought of a friend of mine, who also lived in my same neighborhood. So I invited her to join me in this endeavor, and she agreed. We walked door to door throughout that neighborhood, handing out fliers and personally inviting every woman as we introduced ourselves as neighbors. As the front door would open to each house, I—being a little nosey—noticed the many gods displayed in their living rooms. Asian gods were displayed on pedestals, surrounded by burning candles and fruit offerings that were brought to that god on a daily basis by those in that home to ward off evil spirits. Many Catholic idols were in the yards and porches, and we encountered absolute godless homes, which obviously served the god of this world. It came to me one day that we were fulfilling the Great Commission right in our backyard, "Go ye therefore, and teach all nations" (Matthew 28:19). All nations were represented right there in my neighborhood.

Our six-week neighborhood Bible study turned into a two-year Bible study as God blessed our obedience and brought several ladies every week to my house for a time of singing, worship, and a *Search for Truth* Bible study. The group consisted of Catholics, Baptists, Buddhists, Jews, and some who had never stepped foot inside a church. It was not easy every week, preparing for a study with five children in the home, but God gave me the strength and the burden to do this. It resulted in several being baptized in the name of Jesus and receiving the gift of the Holy Ghost with the evidence of speaking in other tongues!

God will test you with the little things first. He will see if you can be trusted in the small things before the things (that we consider as the big things) are entrusted into our hands. It will be the nursing home service where ten people show up in wheelchairs and fall asleep or shout curse words at each other while you try to teach. It will be behind the counter at the McDonalds or Taco Bell, where you work as you reach for a fellow employee, or maybe at your public high school or college campus, where the Lord is speaking to you about stepping out and starting a Christian club. He will see if you will heed His voice and obey when no one is around to give you credit, no one is there to sing your praises, and no one acknowledges your work. The Lord will test your character to see if you're in it for the praise that comes from man or for the approval of an unseen God, and it's not just a one-time battle because the flesh will try to rise over and over again, desperately wanting to be recognized and acknowledged. It's especially hard because you are swimming upstream against a social media current and an opportunity at every corner to "toot your own horn." Just remember, God keeps good records, and if He can trust you in the small seasons, He can trust you in the bigger seasons.

> Whoever can be trusted with very little can also be trusted with much. (Luke 16:10, NIV)

There is a story that I read periodically in the Book of I Kings that makes me weep every time I read it. There was once a mighty man of God—Scripture only identifies him with that—who had a powerful,

244 | For Women Who Are Called by Women Who Have Answered

prophetic ministry. God used him mightily to prophesy destruction on Jeroboam's altar of idolatry.

The Lord had spoken to this man of God, instructing him not to eat bread or drink water on his journey nor to travel back on the same road by which he came. After using the man and confirming His power in miraculous ways, the Lord sent an old prophet to test his level of obedience. But notice this: his level of obedience was tested in a place when he was weary and weak in his body.

> Their father asked them, "Which way did he go?" And his sons showed him which road the man of God from Judah had taken. So he said to his sons, "Saddle the donkey for me." And when they had saddled the donkey for him, he mounted it and rode after the man of God. He found him sitting under an oak tree and asked, "Are you the man of God who came from Judah?" (I Kings 13:12–14, NIV)

No doubt, this man of God had become exhausted and weary from giving himself to the orders he had received from the Lord. Nothing can warp your ability to hear the voice of God like a weary spirit and a weary body. This man of God, who had just been used so powerfully mere hours before, was in a vulnerable place and didn't even recognize it. He recognized the temptation when he was in the court of the enemy, for the king extended the offer for him to come to his house and to have dinner with him, which also included a gift. It's always easy to pass the test when you're in the house of your enemy. It's easy to be strong when your spirit is alert to your surroundings, but the true test of loyalty is when your guard is down and your spirit is weary.

> So the prophet said to him, "Come home with me and eat." The man of God said, "I cannot turn back and go with you, nor can I eat bread or drink water with you in this place. I have been told by the word of the LORD: 'You must not eat bread or drink water there or return by the way you came.'" (I Kings 13:15–17, NIV)

The old prophet said an angel had appeared to him and told him it was now all right for him to eat since he was a prophet as well. Everything this old prophet asked him to do made sense. Everything the old prophet said was offered at a time when that man of God was weary and in an uncomfortable place. He was hungry, he was hot, and he was thirsty after proclaiming the word of the Lord. He was at a place of exhaustion. It *made sense* for him to eat and drink. And hey! He had just seen great miracles through his ministry; he just watched the king's withered hand stretch forth as brand new!

Here in the valley of logic and weariness, the spirit of confusion came, and he made a choice that was the demise of his ministry. God was testing him through this old prophet to see how much He could truly trust this young man of God. The end of the story brought death to that young man because he "defied the word of the LORD" and did not keep God's command (I Kings 13:21, NIV). A lion met him on his way home and left his body lying on the road.

What a wasted life and wasted ministry all because someone listened to logic when things got uncomfortable for him! I have cried many tears over this story, asking God to make me careful when I become weary. I want God to help me always to see clearly and to stay obedient to the call no matter what temptations come or what would be more pleasing and appetizing to my flesh. No matter how powerfully the anointing is allowed to flow through me, no matter how many miracles and healings I witness, make me careful.

If that young man of God would have held strong to what the Spirit of the Lord originally spoke to his spirit, he may have been the Elijah God was raising up for that day. This man's ministry resembled the way God used the prophet Elijah, and Elijah himself did not come to the scene until later. Heeding the voice of the Lord is a serious thing. It can also be a dangerous thing when it is not taken seriously or with great fear, awe, and complete obedience.

As I write this I feel a strong witness of the Holy Ghost sweeping over me. I feel as if someone reading this needs to heed the Word of the Lord that has been spoken into your life. It is not just a fleeting moment in time that changes with the wind or circumstances; the call of God goes forth without restraint when He makes the choice of whom He wants to use in His kingdom! It is indeed the highest honor but at the same time requires extreme dedication—especially in the dry seasons.

The thing about seasons is that they will eventually change. The doors of ministry will open to you in

God's timing, but until then seek relationship with the Lord and put your hand to the plow wherever you are and whatever season you are in right now. God keeps good records!

8 | *The Priority of the Call*

It happened to me in the summer of 2006. A long, dirt road that was surrounded by walnut and cherry orchards separated our house from the main road, and this was my place to walk each evening. This particular summer, I had been secretly struggling with inner feelings of low self-worth, and to help the violin of pity play even louder, I had just read a note from a friend, telling me of all the doors of ministry the Lord had opened for her. It was not that I was jealous (okay, maybe I was a little jealous). I was honestly happy that God was using her, but it helped the spotlight of inadequacy shine even brighter on my own life. I felt like I wasn't doing anything productive, and to be completely honest with you, I felt trapped. And even worse is what I felt trapped by . . . I felt tied down by my kids. I had five young children who literally consumed my life and demanded a great amount of my time.

Something inside of me kept screaming that I needed to be *out*. I wanted to be out ministering to others, traveling, speaking, leading, helping others, and doing things "for God" I saw others my age doing, but I felt limited by the needs of my five kids. But the fact was, nobody really knew I felt that way. Or so I thought.

The California sunsets are all beautiful on summer evenings, but this one I will never forget. During my evening walk I was about halfway down the road, facing our house, when unexpectedly the Lord Jesus spoke clearly into my spirit. Out of the blue came this question: "Do you really want to please Me?" To say the least, it caught me by surprise and really caught me off guard. I responded as if I were having a conversation, "Well, of course I want to please You, Lord! I have given You my life. I walk with You every day, I pray, I do my best always to obey, and I witness to others about You. What do You mean?"

Friend, if I have *ever* heard the voice of the Lord, I heard it that day walking down the dirt road. God wasn't finished. "Kim, if you truly want to please Me, look straight ahead." As I looked down the road, I saw my five precious kids playing in the front yard: making forts and playing with sticks and their imaginations. We didn't have much of a yard then, but they knew how to build forts with long sticks, they made fire pits with rocks, and they knew how to use their imaginations as they played with one another. Believe me; you could hear them a mile away!

"I have given you five children. If you truly want to please Me, then *they are your ministry.*" I wish I could tell you that I ran down the road with pure excitement and a new burden. No, I will tell you what I did. I stood there and cried. As the tears ran down my face, my eyes were opened, and I felt so ashamed as the Lord made me take an honest look at what I had labeled "ministry." Underneath that mask was the brutal reality of selfishness and a self-seeking mentality; not a drop of it was God.

To say the least, that day on the dirt road forever changed my perspective of ministry. It made me take an honest look at myself, my motives, and the person I *really was* inside. Many things were changed, rearranged, and cancelled in the life of Kim Haney. It doesn't really matter what the world thinks about you, what your church thinks about you, what your peers think about you, or even what you think about yourself. All that matters is that you please Jesus, and many times that includes taking the low road that is less recognized. I have learned from the choices I made that day that doing what the Lord desires always brings much contentment, peace, and fulfillment into one's life. From that day on the dirt road, my children became my first and foremost congregation; they became my ministry!

God knew something that day that I did not. The soil of their hearts was prepared to receive certain spiritual seeds during those younger years, and if that window of opportunity was passed, the soil would begin to change with time and would not be as receptive as it once was. When they reach thirteen to fourteen years of age, I have noticed the seasons begin to change as their wings begin to spread and prepare them for flight. This is a natural process, but thank God for the wake-up call that day on the dirt road. There

He made me aware of the small window of time God granted to plant seeds of doctrine into their spirits.

If you are a young woman who feels a call of ministry upon your life, and if you decide to get married and have children, those kids become your first and foremost calling. Jochebed, the mother of Moses, had Moses only during the preschool years. Trust me, I know these are not easy times; those are the years you can hardly wait to send those precious babies off to school! Jochebed had influence upon Moses between the ages of four and six, but what she did with that time made the difference in that boy's life. She understood the spiritual secret of teaching her young child and catching that window of opportunity, as the doctrinal seeds that were planted into him grew stronger than the pull and allure of the Kingdom of Egypt. No matter what may pull and bid for your children's souls, the Word of God you place inside them while they are young will "stand forever" according to Isaiah 40:8. The promise belongs to us regarding our children if we make it our priority.

I began to ask the Lord when, and how, and what to do. First, He told me to teach them how to pray and to instill the early-morning prayer habit into their lives. I didn't know how that would fly at first, getting them up fifteen minutes earlier before school for prayer, but they did it. I did not have to drag them out of bed every morning for this; they were always excited about their prayer and Bible study time. They actually looked forward to our prayer time in the mornings!

Now, I'm not going to lie to you and say that *every morning* my kids were sweet, happy little angels who quickly jumped out of bed for their prayer time. We had our mornings . . . . We'll just leave it at that! The devotional time brought a sense of fulfillment to their days as they left for school, but it also brought a fulfillment to me, knowing I was operating in the ministry God had appointed for that moment in time.

Second, He began to show me that I needed to teach them the truths of the Word of God. So I started with a *Search For Truth II* color chart. That summer, when they were out of school, we would get the chart out and I would teach them from it. They loved the pictures of the people and beasts in Hell when the Revelation study began, and they would ask questions from the other pictures they saw. I deeply encourage you to do this with your kids. You don't have to be a seminary teacher to teach it. Out of this experience came my first book, *Seeds of Jochebed,* which is a compilation of Bible lessons I taught my kids before they went to school each morning. I never would have dreamed of writing a book, but looking back I can see: from that test of obedience flowed other avenues of ministry.

Most of my children are now grown, young adults, and I look back on the past in absolute amazement and gratitude to God for giving me a good, straight talk at the time it mattered most. He exposed all the ugly pride and arrogance that slyly resided behind the camouflaged front of acceptance and revealed it for what it really was.

Whether you are a woman who has a call of God upon your life or not, *every mother* has a call to teach her children the Word of God. To sum it up: If you are a mother, you have a calling from God. You have a calling upon your life just like Moses, David, Deborah, Esther, and countless others did. If you are a mother, God's call and will for you is to be a mother. If you will ever know the feeling of God being with you and His anointing resting upon you, it will come when you minister to your children. I wouldn't allow society or the culture to rob me of the greatest opportunity on the face of the earth. I would downsize to a smaller home, drive an older car, make sacrificial financial choices, or whatever was necessary to be present and effective in the lives of my kids while they were young. It wouldn't matter if the whole world stood against me or made me feel inferior because of my choices; it will all be worth it on that great day when I stand before the throne. Every effort I have made will be rewarded when my family circle stands unbroken in Heaven and I have the satisfaction of knowing I have done the will of God.

President Theodore Roosevelt made this powerful statement about motherhood:

> When all is said, it is the mother, and the mother only, who is a better citizen than the soldier who fights for his country. The successful mother, the mother who does her part in rearing and training aright the boys and girls who are to be the men and women of the next generation is of greater use to the community, and occupies, if she would

only realize it, a more honorable as well as a more important position than any man in it. The mother is the one supreme asset of the national life. She is more important, by far, than the successful statesman, or businessman, or artist or scientist.

Because a mother and grandmother understood the importance of making their children their first ministry, Timothy was produced. Paul understood that this powerful young minister was the product of a mother and grandmother who were dedicated to their first calling:

> But you [Timothy] must continue in the things which you have learned and been assured of, knowing from whom you have learned them, and that from childhood [this signals to us who it was that taught him these things] you have known the Holy Scriptures, which are able to make you wise for salvation through faith which is in Christ Jesus. (II Timothy 3:14–15, NKJV)

To whom was Paul referring in verse 14 when he said, "knowing from whom you learned it"? He referred to Eunice and Lois, Timothy's mother and grandmother. Paul understood that many of the foundations that were built in Timothy happened during his childhood teaching. Earlier Paul made mention of the faith that was handed to Timothy from his mother and grandmother:

> When I call to remembrance the genuine faith that is in you, which dwelt first in your grandmother Lois and your mother Eunice, and I am persuaded is in you also. (II Timothy 1:5, NKJV)

Timothy's father was never referred to as being a spiritual implementer in his life. When Paul chose Timothy to be his missionary partner, he said this about the young man's father:

> Then he came to Derbe and Lystra. And behold, a certain disciple was there, named Timothy, the son of a certain Jewish woman who believed, but his father was Greek. (Acts 16:1, NKJV)

Timothy was the product of a home with a believing mother and an unbelieving father. That is why Timothy did not learn the Scriptures from his father. His father did not believe them, but his mother did. No matter what your situation, God will use a dedicated mother who is willing to take the time to pour into her children. And it is not a matter of option, but it is a command of God to minister first to your husband and children, before anything or anyone else.

> That they may teach the young women to be sober, to love their husbands, to love their children, to be discreet, chaste, keepers at home, good, obedient to their own husbands, that the word of God be not blasphemed. (Titus 2:4–5)

Linda Gleason, president of Ladies Ministries of the United Pentecostal Church International, has a deep passion for women to understand the importance of their role in the home as mothers and wives. I am deeply moved by what she writes regarding the topic, keepers at home:

Is there a greater calling than walking through the valley of the shadow of death to give life to one of the greatest miracles God has ever created, the human being? Is there a greater calling than to mold and set that life on course for generations to come, until Jesus comes or the world ends? Is there a greater calling than to leave a legacy that will never die? Is there a greater calling than to influence the lives of all the future generations of your family tree?

There are brilliant women who have brilliant careers. They impact their companies. They do great and marvelous things. But the day they walk out of the company after a farewell gathering where words of appreciation, commendation, and applause are spoken and beautiful gifts are given, their influence will be overshadowed by another, and their name gradually becomes unknown.

But motherhood! Oh great, noble motherhood! You devote your life for the period of years in rearing your children—establishing their future in God and in life. You set a course for generations of human beings who will never cease to exist. Your grandchildren will speak of you. Your great-grandchildren will speak of you. The impact of the years that you devote to rearing your children will live forever!

Was it important for the Israelites to be freed from Egypt after about four hundred years of bondage and life under the cruel torment of Pharaoh's taskmasters day after interminable day with no end in sight? Absolutely yes! But not without their children. Pharaoh's little bargaining ploy for them to go but leave the children was not even a question. They would choose to stay and be slaves rather than leave Egypt without their children! God honored their commitment, and when Israel marched out of Egypt, families went together—parents and kids!

God sees the heart of a mother. When Hannah longed for a child, she made her way to the temple, where she poured out her soul in agony. Her actions were misinterpreted by the high priest until he understood her plight. Then he pronounced her miracle: she would have a child. Only a few years later she presented her miracle back to God. From the lips of a child came a rebuke to the priest who would not take authority over his household. Eli's sons flung degradation and sin in the eyes of God on the porch of the temple, but the influence of a mother in just a few short years put into the heart of the little boy, Samuel, the ability to hear the voice of the Lord and to speak without fear the word given. This produced the ability to manifest a love for God and a dedication to God that prepared him to lead Israel as one of its greatest prophets.

Jochebed was another amazing mother, whom we read about in the Bible and admire, who had just a few short years of raising her son to the weaning stage. She put into the heart of Moses a love for God, for the people of God, and for the ways of God that held him in good stead when every temptation that has ever faced mankind flew into his face. Yet he stood for what was in his heart, put there by his mother. He gave up fame. He gave up fortune. He gave up title. He gave up position. He gave up authority. He chose suffering. He chose humility. Moses chose to follow what his mother put into his heart rather than take the throne of leadership in the most powerful nation of his world.

Motherhood is a noble calling for women of all times. The ability to influence lives for generations to come is one of the greatest powers on earth. God established the family, and it was established even before the church. It is the fiber and core of strong nations and strong churches. Strong families are the enemy's greatest nightmare. That is why, down through the ages, he has eroded and attacked the strength of the family.

Where are the mothers of the twenty-first century? The needs of the child are more than clean clothes, a warm bed, a full tummy, and a good education. Greater than the physical needs are the emotional and spiritual needs of a little one growing up in a confusing and wicked world. Two to three hours per week for a child in the church house is not enough time to tie the spiritual chords so tightly in their lives that they will never be broken. Faithfulness to the house of God is paramount. It is the command of Scripture, "Not forsaking the assembling of ourselves together, as the manner of some is; but exhorting one another: and so much the more, as ye see the day approaching" (Hebrews 10:25). We in the twenty-first century know that the day is approaching quickly.

As important as the church, as critical as the relationship of the pastor's influence in the life of a child, the home is the place where the strength of godliness as well as love and passion for the kingdom of God and the Word is birthed, fed, nurtured, and solidified. Three hours of church per week cannot override thirty-five to forty hours of bombardment upon the mind of a child with the philosophies of men and wickedness of the world. This does not even include the influence of twenty to thirty hours of social media, entertainment, and technology.

Who is rearing the children of our generation? Who is fulfilling the mandate of Deuteronomy 6:4–7:

> Hear, O Israel: The LORD our God is one LORD: and thou shalt love the LORD thy God with all thine heart, and with all thy soul, and with all thy might. And these words, which I command thee this day, shall be in thine heart: and thou shalt teach them diligently unto thy children, and shalt talk of them when thou sittest in thine house, and when thou walkest by the way, and when thou liest down, and when thou risest up.

It sounds like a time-consuming job, this everyday, all-day guideline to parental teaching. Could it be that the Jewish culture has remained strong over thousands of years because of those principles mandated by God in their earliest history? How many generations will the Apostolic Pentecostal movement survive if those principles are thrown aside because times have changed and mothers have left the rearing of their children to other entities?

It is interesting to note the admonition of Paul in Titus 2:3–5:

> The aged women likewise, that they be in behaviour as becometh holiness, not false accusers, not given to much wine, teachers of good things; that they may teach the young women to be sober, to love their husbands, to love their children, to be discreet, chaste, keepers at home, good, obedient to their own husbands, that the word of God be not blasphemed.

It wasn't likely that the general rule during those times was that a young woman with children would not be at home taking care of the family and household. Perhaps the passage may have more significance to our times than Paul's times. I know we women of today are the proverbial "super women"! We can work a forty-hour week, not counting overtime, with a one- to two-hour commute per day, make sure the children are cared for, take care of meals, laundry, cleaning, church involvement, and attendance plus a few of the children's extracurricular activities, have family time and devotions, teach our children the Word, hear their joys and sorrows, and have time for family interaction. We can do it all! We can handle it! Who are we trying to fool?

A child has one childhood. It is lived a day at a time. Every day brings a new experience, a new memory, a little piece of joy filed in the bank of *things I will always cherish*. When it is over, it is over. It can never be reclaimed. Life moves onward, never backward. A few years of a mother's life devoted to raising her children will be some of her most precious lifelong memories, and a whole lifetime is left to pursue other interests, goals, and accomplishments.

Rearing a child in the fear and admonition of the Lord takes time. Other than God and family, time in our twenty-first century is the most valuable commodity we have. It is more valuable than money. The enemy has sneaked into our homes and stolen our family time. We live such busy lives that we rarely can sit down and enjoy a family meal together. Even if we do, too often it is accompanied by electronic devices that inhibit family interaction, conversation, sharing, and strengthening.

During World War II, when things were looking bleak for England, Sir Winston Churchill made a speech that inspired and empowered the English nation and her military to face the impossible with fire in their blood. He said:

> You ask, what is our aim? I can answer in one word: It is victory, victory at all costs, victory in spite of all terror, victory, however long and hard the road may be; for without victory, there is no survival. . . . We shall go on to the end, we shall fight in France, we shall fight on the seas and oceans, we shall fight with growing confidence and growing strength in the air, we shall defend our Island, whatever the cost may be, we shall fight on the beaches, we shall fight on the landing grounds, we shall fight in the fields and in the streets, we shall fight in the hills; we shall never surrender.

Fight they did until the bloody end, and they got their victory! I say that needs to be the cry and determination of the hearts of mothers in our times. We will fight for our children. We will fight the battle for time, we will fight the influence of media, we will fight the influence of fame, and we will fight philosophies of men. We will never give up! Our goal is to go to Heaven. I say, moms, that our goal needs to be: "Not without my children!" We need strong, godly women in our world who will not be ashamed to spend a portion of their lives being a keeper at home!

A few years ago, a lady minister showed up at our church in Stockton. I did not know this person and had never met her before, but just as we do with everyone, we welcomed her and made her feel at home. One day she caught me while I was at the church and asked me if she could possibly minister to the college students or speak in one of their chapel services. Well, to be completely honest with you, there was a red flag right there. Just the fact she would ask without first an invitation sent signals that something was not quite right. I was kind but politely stated the calendar had already been filled.

I later found out this lady had been gone from home for several weeks on an evangelistic mission and left her husband and young children at home. My friends, something is not right with this picture, and now I understand why there was a red flag in my spirit when she approached me. I don't see scripturally how God's favor and anointing could rest upon a woman when she was willing to leave her first priority, which is her husband and her children, for weeks at a time and follow some path that has been labeled as "ministry." Those things have a time and a season if God ordains them for your life, but if you step out of your season and try to attain things that are not meant for that particular season, you will create voids that can never be refilled or repaired. Doors of ministry that may cause you to be away from your home will open for you *in their season*. There is a great danger in trying to push these doors open before their time.

The late J. T. Pugh, one of the greatest men of God who ever walked the earth, in my opinion, was a master at training young ministers. He spent several of his years mentoring and training young men and women for the ministry. I want to share a thought I heard him teach that explains the importance of accepting and making the most of the season you are in:

> Our lives are made up of seasons and each season has its beginning and end. It is important that we finish out those seasons completely so there is no gap, for if there is, our lives will never be what they ought to be. We need to do well and embrace the season we find ourselves in, for these are the particular seasons we are responsible for.
>
> Life is a series of shelves and each shelf holds the things that belong on that shelf. We are supposed to go from experiencing things on one level to the next level, but if we crowd life and try to skip a shelf and jump from shelf A to shelf C, and try to skip the shelves in between, it will affect our lives and ministry because there are experiences in every season of life that all of us need to endure in order to become mature. There may be some particular items that belong in this season of life you are in right now that could be really allowed to influence and mold you, but having your mind-set on shelf C will cause you to miss something, and you can never go back and get what you missed in those seasons. There are particular seasons of life that are ordained and set forth by God, and it makes a huge difference when you can correctly put into that season what needs to be done.
>
> I have seen people rise to particular seasons of life and they seem totally unprepared for it. They were devastated because the expectations they confronted at that particular stage of life were too much for them, and they were not able to cope

with it. Why? Because there were some things not taken care of earlier that were deeply laid in the very psychic of their being.

The enemy will use the mask of "ministry opportunities" to tempt a person—either man or woman. I can think of a family or two in which the mother and father sold out to the church but failed to minister first in the home to their children, and now the children want nothing to do with God. Let us realize as mothers that our first calling is to train our children while they are young. We must take advantage of this short season so we can look back with no regrets, knowing we did the will of God for that season of life. The church cannot do this, the Sunday school cannot do this. Christian schools, clubs, youth groups, nothing will have the ability to speak into your child's life like a mother.

God thought it was so important the way a parent raised his children that Abraham's entire calling was due to the fact the Lord knew he would instruct and train his children to serve the one true, living God:

> For I know him [Abraham], that he will command his children and his household after him, and they shall keep the way of the Lord, to do justice and judgment; that the Lord may bring upon Abraham that which he hath spoken of him. (Genesis 18:19, NKJV)

God knew He could trust Abraham with the responsibility of ministering to and training his children first to love and to serve the Lord. This action was so vital that his calling hinged upon it!

Linda Gleason shares these closing remarks on the power of a mother:

> Home. The mere mention of the word floods the heart with memories as we take a journey back through the private, personal path that leads into the world of yesterday. The school bus topping over that last hill. Walking down the long driveway with the smell of homemade bread wafting through the open windows. The sounds of "family" around the kitchen table as events of the day were relived. Things such as sympathy for Sissy's humiliation in the classroom; indignation at inequities against Little Brother on the playground; empathy for Baby's miserable cold; pride in Dad's promotion; laughter at the "gum in the hair" fiasco. It's not a "linens, china, crystal, steak, and shrimp" dinner, just beef stew and bread on mismatched crockery. But around that table, the strong and lasting fabric of "home" was woven—thread by thread, day after day. We were safe. We were protected. We were home. But it didn't happen by chance.
>
> The *keeper* ordered the atmosphere. When she smiled, the house rang with laughter. When she lay sick, there was a shroud of silence and tension. Her kiss soothed the pain of the hurt. The sound of her singing was security to her offspring. Her prayers rang in the ears of the children. Her support, submission, and love made Dad strong and proud to be the household leader. Mom was the *keeper of the home*.
>
> Thus the home of yesteryear proceeded merrily on its way, giving strength to the nation, stability to the church, security to the children, and satisfaction to the parents.
>
> Until . . . infiltration!

Silently, stealthily, without announcement and fanfare, the easily accessible evil of the end time tried to make its way into our homes. Oh, it didn't proclaim itself as a dark and monstrous beast, breathing fire, uttering profanity from its pernicious throat. No, it came innocently, sugarcoated and glittering in the form of toys, games, books, magazines, posters, and music. It came sneaking into the corners and crevices of our homes through the eye-gate and ear-gate of every soul, stealing the minds of the children. It came intelligently, logically, and skillfully in the form of bigger and better things, prestigious jobs, busier lifestyles, and important activities. Creatively and cunning it came creeping into the schedules of parents, stealing their time.

Suddenly, we looked around. Gone were the family times around the kitchen table. Instead, there were independent individuals occupying the same household, behind closed doors, going separate ways at different times, all seeking to fulfill themselves but lacking the needed support of one another. Gone were the carefree days of childhood, when the biggest problem was listening for the supper bell and making sure you were washed up and at the table on time. Gone were the days when a kid awoke in the early morning cold and snuggled deeper under the quilts as he listened to the comforting sounds of Mom getting Dad off to work or the voices of Mom and Dad praying. Instead there was "wonderful" technology, modern conveniences, bigger and better homes, fascinating and intriguing entertainment, faster cars, accessible air travel—everything for comfort and ease, fun and frolic! And with that change birthed children who suffer from childhood stress, abuse, neglect, insecurity, and worry. It birthed children who worry whether Mommy and Daddy love each other and will stay together, children who worry about their safety in the schoolhouse and even safety in their own homes, children who wonder if anyone really cares. The fabric was unraveling. Security was gone and home wasn't safe anymore.

Until . . . revelation!

The keeper arose, pushed through the cob-webbed cares of life, straightened her armor and began the march through her household against evil. On her knees, Mom began to claim and reclaim anything that may have been lost through infiltration of the enemy. The threads were caught up and mended, and weaving began again in earnest.

Has it happened in every home? No. Should we suspect that the enemy will try to attack our home? Absolutely! It matters not to him your name, your position, your financial standing, or your heritage. If there is any crack or cranny for entrance, he'll arrive to steal, kill, and destroy. He would like nothing better than to wreck the children and devastate the strength and harmony of the family. But we are not "ignorant of his devices." By the grace of God, armed with the Word of God, leaning on the power of prayer, moms will stand at the door with spiritual antennas scanning whatever crosses the threshold. We will fight through schedules and activities for "family time," and with the help of the Lord, we will win!

On guard, Mom, keep the home!

As a mother and woman of God with a call of God upon her life, my first priority is my family and children. No one can take my place in the lives of my children, and what an incredible opportunity to know I am affecting their lives for eternity!

If you are a mother with a call of God upon your life, teach your children how to fall in love with Jesus by the example they see in the home every day. Let them hear you pray in the early morning hours; make your home a haven of worship by playing worship music throughout your home or preached messages through the hallways. They may laugh or make comments, but, Mother, you're doing your job by keeping them centered upon the Lord. And if you don't do it, no one else will.

I pray over every mother reading this book right now that in the name of Jesus there would be a covering over her home, her marriage, and her children. Let there be an awakening to the huge responsibility that rests upon her shoulders, and may she rise to accept this calling. I pray for a great anointing that would descend upon her as she teaches her children, fulfilling the call of God, and plants within them the unwavering seeds of truth. In Jesus' name!

Notes

1. Charles Spurgeon, *Lectures to my Students* (Peabody, MA: Hendrickson Publishers Marketing, LLC, fourth printing 2014), 46–47.

2. Leonard Ravenhill, *Why Revival Tarries* (Bloomington, Minnesota: Bethany House Publishers, 1959), 19.

3. Kim Haney, *Christians and Strongholds* (Stockton, California: Women of the Spirit Publications, 2011), 34.

4. Watchman Nee, *The Normal Christian Life* (Bombay, India: Gospel Literature Service, 1957), 145–48.

5. Bobbye Wendell's experience at the altar in the leper chapel can also be found in the closing pages of *Acts: I Will Build My Church* (Global Association of Theological Studies, 2015) and in *Apostolic Heroes in Global Missions,* Dorsey Burk, ed. (Hazelwood, MO: Word Aflame Press, 2016).

6. Watchman Nee, *Authority and Submission* (Anaheim, California: Living Stream Ministry, 1988), 192.

7. R. T. Kendall, *Total Forgiveness* (Lake Mary, Florida: Charisma House Publishers, 1973), xxiv.